# Managing Mixed Financing of Privately Owned Providers in the Public Interest

**Judith Smith, Nicholas Mays,
Crispin Ovenden, Jacqueline Cumming,
Janet McDonald, and Jonathan Boston**

Institute of Policy Studies

First printed in 2010


Institute of Policy Studies
School of Government
Victoria University of Wellington
PO Box 600
Wellington


© Institute of Policy Studies
ISBN 978-1-877347-39-9
IPS/Pub/168

*Copy-editor: Belinda Hill*
*Cover design: Milne Print*


Printed by Milne Print

# Contents

# Figure

# Tables

# Preface

This book sets out the findings of a project that examined how government agencies in New Zealand, Australia, and England finance public services delivered by private providers. The project paid particular attention to 'mixed' financing arrangements (that is, services with both public and private sources of funding). The project took a cross-sectoral and international perspective and focused on:

- general practice (primary health care)
- long-term care of older people
- legal aid
- early childhood education.

The book has six chapters. Chapter 1 outlines the background to, and objectives of, the research. Chapter 2 sets out our conceptual framework, while chapter 3 summarises the financing arrangements for the four services in New Zealand, Australia, and England. This discussion is used in chapter 4 as the basis for a typology of approaches to the mixed financing of public services. The research team applied the typology to the four areas in the three countries and identified criteria deemed important when considering a particular mix of public and private finance for a service. These criteria are outlined in a proposed assessment framework in chapter 5. The framework is intended for use by policy makers when they are deciding on a particular approach to mixed financing. The framework assesses mixed financing from the three perspectives of the state, providers, and users.

In chapter 6 we conclude the book and suggest five issues to be addressed when a mixed financing approach is used for public services The issues are the:

- role of mixed financing in ensuring access, quality, and value for money
- importance of context
- extent and nature of contracting
- significance of user charges
- nature of user involvement and control.

# Acknowledgments

The authors are extremely grateful to a large number of people for their assistance with this book and the project of which the book was a part. We would like to thank the Emerging Issues Project of the Institute of Policy Studies in the School of Government at Victoria University of Wellington for funding the project.

We would also like to thank all those who were interviewed for the project, who attended a workshop held on the project, who responded to requests for information from us, and who commented on drafts. We very much appreciate the time you all committed to this work and for the goodwill shown throughout the project. The research assistance of Colin Barr is also gratefully acknowledged.

All errors and omissions, of course, remain the responsibility of the authors.

# Contributors

**Judith Smith** is Head of Policy at the Nuffield Trust in London. Judith is an experienced and widely published health services researcher and policy analyst. Before joining the Nuffield Trust in February 2009, she spent 14 years working at the Health Services Management Centre, University of Birmingham, as a senior lecturer and the Director of Research. Before that, Judith was a senior manager in the National Health Service and successfully completed the National Health Service Management Training Scheme. At the Nuffield Trust, Judith's research focuses on the role and potential of physician groups, the development of commissioning in the National Health Service, and the quest for health system efficiency in the economic downturn. From 2007 to 2009, Judith undertook a research fellowship at Victoria University of Wellington in New Zealand. She was also a visiting academic fellow in the New Zealand Ministry of Health, where she acted as an adviser on primary care reform, and a visiting fellow at the Australian Primary Health Care Research Institute in Canberra.

**Nicholas Mays** is Professor of Health Policy and Head of the Department of Health Services Research and Policy at the London School of Hygiene and Tropical Medicine, University of London. He also heads the Health Services Research Unit. Since 2003, Nicholas has spent about three months each year as a policy adviser to the New Zealand Ministry of Health and the State Sector Performance Branch of The Treasury, New Zealand. From 1998 to 2003, he was principal adviser in the Health and Cross-Sector Strategy sections in the Social Policy Branch of The Treasury. From 1994 to 1998, he was Director of Health Services Research at the King's Fund, London. From 1991 to 1993, he directed the Health and Health Care Research Unit in the Queen's University of Belfast. Before then, he held a variety of research posts in the Universities of London (St Thomas's Hospital Medical School) and Leicester, government agencies, and the National Health Service.

**Crispin Ovenden** is a medical student at the University of Otago. He worked as a research fellow at the Health Services Research Centre in the School of Government, Victoria University of Wellington in 2007 and 2008. From 2002 to 2006, Crispin worked as an economist in the Monetary Analysis Department at the Bank of England where he prepared analyses and quarterly forecasts of euro-area economies. From 2000 to 2002, Crispin worked as a business analyst in the Banking and Market Service Department of the Bank of England where he reviewed tariff structure policy for high value payment systems.

**Jacqueline Cumming** is Director of the Health Services Research Centre in the School of Government, Victoria University of Wellington. She has extensive public policy experience, having worked for several New Zealand government policy organisations, including the Ministry of Health, before joining the Health Services Research Centre. Jacqueline also coordinates School of Government courses on health policy and monitoring and evaluation and supervises doctoral and masters students. Her research interests are in priority setting, access to health services, primary health care and health systems reform, and evaluation. Jacqueline has led several high-profile projects in recent years, including a national evaluation of the Primary Health Care Strategy and a national evaluation of New Zealand's Healthy Eating – Healthy Action Strategy, and is involved in projects exploring economic and productivity issues in New Zealand health care. Jacqueline is president of the Health Services Research Association of Australia and New Zealand.

**Janet McDonald** is a research fellow at the Health Services Research Centre in the School of Government, Victoria University of Wellington. She has worked on evaluations of the 2001 New Zealand health reforms, the implementation of the Primary Health Care Strategy, and the Healthy Eating – Healthy Action Strategy. Her research interests also include informal care-giving.

**Jonathan Boston** is Professor of Public Policy and Director of the Institute of Policy Studies in the School of Government, Victoria University of Wellington. He has published widely on public management, social policy, tertiary education, comparative government, and New Zealand politics.

# 1

# Introduction

In 2007, the Health Services Research Centre at Victoria University of Wellington was awarded funding through the Emerging Issues Programme.[1] The funding was for an exploratory project to examine how government agencies in New Zealand, Australia, and England finance services delivered by private providers, in particular 'mixed' financing arrangements (that is, services with both public and private sources of funding). The project takes a cross-sectoral and international perspective and focuses on general practice (primary health care), long-term care of older people, legal aid, and early childhood education. The book identifies several issues policy makers face when they seek to develop or extend mixed financing approaches to meet policy objectives, develops a typology for thinking about the options involved in designing mixed financing policies, and suggests a set of criteria against which to assess key policy options.

## Aims and objectives

The aim of this project was to examine the issues associated with developing and implementing mixed financing arrangements and, in particular, to learn from recent experience in different areas of New Zealand public policy and from international comparisons about the strengths and weaknesses of different approaches to the mixed financing of public services. Specifically, the project objectives were to:

- identify the range of approaches relating to mixed financing of private providers within different settings in New Zealand: general

---

1    Emerging Issues Projects resulted from a decision in 2006 by chief executives in the public sector to pool funds to enable the Institute of Policy Studies to conduct research on longer-term issues of cross-cutting significance to the whole of the public sector.

practice (primary health care), long-term care for older people, legal aid, and early childhood education

- identify approaches to financing similar services in Australia and England
- explore some of the reasons for the different ways of financing services in these four service areas, drawing together New Zealand and international experience
- examine the rationale for the mix of user charges and public finance of private providers in these service areas in both the New Zealand and international context.
- develop a framework to explore the advantages and disadvantages of different forms of mixed financing of services, from user, provider and state perspectives, taking account of contextual differences between New Zealand, Australia and England
- examine recent policy issues that have arisen related to the New Zealand, Australian, and English experience of mixed financing of private providers
- make recommendations for future policy development and implementation in relation to mixed financing of private providers for specific public services in New Zealand
- scope a larger-scale research project for future funding focused on the implications of using public and private sources to pay private providers to deliver public services.

## Background

### Mixed financing in New Zealand health services policy

This project had its beginnings in New Zealand health services policy. The government continues to be the main financier of health and disability support services in New Zealand, generally contributing around 78% of total expenditure (Ministry of Health, 2008a). The government is also a key provider of services, providing, for example, emergency services; acute and elective hospital services; hospital and community mental health, disability support, and rehabilitation services;

and public health services. Private for-profit and private not-for-profit organisations also provide many services, for example, primary health care, community mental health, and disability support services and residential rest home care.

In recent years, New Zealand's Primary Health Care Strategy (Minister of Health (A King), 2001) has sought to shift government financing of primary health care from a targeted approach to a more universal approach (albeit not fully free at point of use). The government provided some $2.2 billion in new funding to support the strategy during 2002–2008 (Minister of Health (P Hodgson), 2005). A key issue, however, is that privately owned and managed primary health care providers (especially general practitioners (GPs)) sought to retain the right to charge patients fees. This was a source of tension as the government implemented the new funding for primary health care. As a result, various questions arose.

- Should the government continue to grant the right to GPs to charge their patients fees in the presence of a rising share of public funding?

- What is the right balance between user fees and public finance in paying for general practice services?

- Are fee reductions related to the most beneficial general practice services?

- If GPs continue to have the right to charge their patients, how does the government ensure its new funding is allocated to reducing patient fees and improving services rather than simply contributing to an income increase for GPs?

- Is it possible to incentivise providers to keep fees lower than they would otherwise have been in the absence of extra public finance, and if so, how might this be done?

- How can the government monitor the improvements in access and population health that it is getting in return for increasing its funding of general practice services?

- Has the reduction in fees enabled the achievement of the wider population health objectives of the government?

- How could the current policy be modified to enable the maintenance of low fees and the achievement of the other objectives of the Primary Health Care Strategy such as reduced health inequalities?

### *Mixed financing in other areas of public policy*

In thinking about the issues raised above, the research team noted other areas of New Zealand public policy where similar issues arise, but where the arrangements for combining and managing public and private funding differ. For example, the government caps its funding to providers of older people's residential care and sets the amount of co-funding by users. By contrast, the government still permits GPs to set their own fees charged to patients, while recently encouraging GPs through local agreements (rather than regulation) to ensure increases in government funding are passed on to patients in the form of lower patient charges.

In the area of legal aid, the government only provides public funding to lawyers for services for those users who pass an income and assets test.

In education, the government provides funding for 20 hours of free early childhood education to all three- and four-year-olds enrolled in fee-paying, teacher-led care, offers a base subsidy to all licensed places (from the Ministry of Education), and offers a subsidy for childcare to working parents (from Work and Income New Zealand).

The government also caps the fee increases universities can charge students and limits the types of charges that primary and secondary schools can compulsorily seek from families (schools may still seek voluntary donations).

In respect of transport, the government has been exploring the possibility of charging for road use in Auckland and other congested areas of New Zealand.

These examples raise questions as to whether the funding differences have an underlying rationale or have arisen haphazardly (perhaps as a result of political pressures and compromises) and whether the different models offer particular advantages and disadvantages that policy makers should consider when developing policies and programmes.

## Mixed financing as a means of delivering government objectives for the population and service users

The decision by a government to provide partial funding signals the presence of government objectives related to the particular service and a concern by the government to influence service uptake or delivery. Establishing the nature of these objectives is an important prerequisite to establishing a local framework for evaluating different potential approaches to mixed funding, so approaches can be tested for their likely ability to fulfil the government's objectives.

For example, when the government decided to provide funding for 20 hours of free early childhood education for all three- and four-year-olds, this represented an explicit response to the accumulation of longitudinal research evidence about the importance of 'early years' education and of that education being teacher-led (only teacher-led organisations can access the government funding).[2] In this way, government priorities were being emphasised through the offering of a partial subsidy, on a universal basis, to users of private early childhood education.

Government priorities may similarly lead to the part-funding of a service that was previously fully funded by government, as in the case of National Health Service (NHS) eye tests in England. In this case, the government stopped funding free eye tests for all adults and funded only high priority groups (for example, senior citizens and people with a family history of serious eye disease) for free tests. In this way, the government was indicating that it regarded eye tests as not central to the mission of the NHS and/or that eye tests were of limited value in terms of health improvement.

---

2    This excluded playcentres and kōhanga reo, which are parent- and whānau-led. In the May 2009 Budget, the new National-led government announced that the scheme would be extended to cover these two services from July 2010 (Tolley, 2009).

Another example of changing government priorities leading to funding changes is that of general practice services in New Zealand. In the 1940s and 1950s, most of the cost of general practice services was funded by government, but over time the government subsidy level remained the same in nominal terms while the costs of providing and accessing the service increased, leading to the cost of services increasingly falling onto private individuals. As with the NHS example, the New Zealand government too was implicitly indicating that general practice services were of less benefit than other fully funded health services or that such day-to-day services should be the responsibility of individuals rather than the government.

## Methods

The focus of this project is on financing arrangements between public funders and private providers, with the use of co-payments or user charges alongside public funding. Therefore, the research started with a review of New Zealand and international literature on these topics. The literature review included documentary analysis of four public services across New Zealand, Australia, and England where public funding is given to private providers alongside users' contributions: general practice, long-term care for older people, legal aid, and early childhood education.

This brief review of the literature was used to inform a series of semi-structured interviews with senior officials in the relevant government agencies related to the four public policy areas (that is, the Ministries of Health, Education, and Justice) and with organisations that represent the providers of these services (that is, the New Zealand Medical Association, New Zealand Law Society, and New Zealand Early Childhood Council).

The research team then integrated their findings from the literature review and interviews into a discussion document that formed the basis for a workshop held in Wellington in April 2008. The workshop involved policy makers and providers of services in the four policy areas, along with academic colleagues and others deemed to have an interest in the issue of mixed financing of public services. The workshop focused on discussing the typology of mixed financing approaches and exploring how such approaches might be evaluated. The material presented in chapters 4 and 5 build on the discussion and conclusions of the workshop.

In the next chapter, we set out the conceptual approach that underpins this research, along with findings from our review of the literature concerning the use of mixed financing in public services.

# 2

## Conceptual Approach

### Mixed financing of public services

In theory, health, education, legal, and other services can be provided through the market, with consumers paying directly, or through private insurance. However, many governments choose to contribute to the financing or provision of a wide variety of public services for several reasons. The principal reason is to ensure equity of access, but in some situations the reason is to improve efficiency where fully private markets would produce suboptimal effects. This funding and provision can be done in different ways, leading to a range of combinations of public and private finance and provision. The four basic combinations of public–private financing and provision that can be observed are:

- public finance and public provision
- public finance and private provision
- private finance and public provision
- private finance and private provision (Donaldson and Gerard, 2005).

However, more-complex combinations are possible (shared public and private funding, or mixed public and private provision of services). The focus of this book is on the combination of public finance and private provision and private finance and private provision in a single service.

In addition to considering whether particular revenue sources will generate sufficient funds for desired services, policy makers need to consider the impact of different systems and combinations of financing on specific policy objectives. For example, Mossialos et al (2002) ask the following questions.

- Is the funding system progressive (regressive or proportional); that is, does it require those on higher incomes to pay on average more than (less than, the same as) those on lower incomes? And do the benefits of the service accrue disproportionately to one end of the income distribution?

- Is the funding system horizontally equitable; that is, is the financing burden on individuals fairly distributed among those who have the same income?

- Does the funding and provision system result in the redistribution of wealth in a more equal way among the population?

- How does the funding system affect coverage and access to services?

- How does the funding system affect cost containment?

- Does the funding system change consumption behaviour in a way that may lead to over- or under-consumption of some goods at the expense of other meritorious goods?

- How does the funding system affect the wider economy?

- How does the funding system affect allocative and technical efficiency?

In this book, we develop a framework that seeks to enable policy makers to assess a particular mixed financing approach in respect of the types of issues raised above. We propose a set of questions that focus on what we consider the issues associated with a mixed financing approach and the issues participants highlighted in the project workshop.

## Role of user charges in mixed financing of public services

This project examines privately provided and part publicly financed services where users are expected to make some financial contribution to the cost of services in the form of a user charge (that is, a charge over and above what the user might pay for the service through taxation). This approach can be seen in examples such as general practice fees and prescription charges in New Zealand; prescription charges in England; consumer contributions to long-term care in New Zealand, Australia, and England; user contributions to legal aid in Australia; and mixed financing of child care systems in New Zealand and England.

User charges have two main functions in relation to public services: they may generate additional funding for these services and they may reduce demand for these services (Robinson, 2004). Reducing demand may relate to 'moral hazard' arguments, whereby it is asserted that consumers may change their behaviour and be less conscious of containing costs if they are insured or publicly subsidised (Donaldson and Gerard, 2005). In this situation, cost sharing or co-payment by consumers aims to make consumers more aware of the cost of services and thereby reduce 'unnecessary' usage. On the other hand, cost sharing may also discourage the desirable use of services with potentially negative consequences (for example, in terms of equity of access) and increased costs in the longer term.

An examination of the main user charges in the public health care systems of countries such as the United Kingdom, the Netherlands, Sweden, Denmark, France, and Germany shows that charges are relatively common but very variable, with their existence and political acceptability often a function of how a particular health service has evolved in an individual country rather than an expression of underlying ideology or explicit rationale (Robinson, 2004). User charges typically raise only modest amounts of revenue and are not a significant deterrent for the more affluent parts of the population, and exemptions are often made for key groups such as children and the elderly so they are not discouraged from seeking necessary services (Robinson, 2004). This raises questions as to the purpose of user charges within a country's health system, apart from containing public spending.

An important part of the historical explanation for the extent to which state funders use private providers and the extent of public finance is how a particular profession (for example, general practice, hospital medicine, dentistry, law, or teaching) or service sector (for example, early childhood education or long-term care) developed its relationship with the state during the formative years of the welfare state in the 1930s and 1940s. Thus, public hospital services in New Zealand became fully publicly financed from the 1940s, but hospital specialists were permitted to have parallel private practices. With general practitioners, the state initially subsidised all patients at a fixed rate at the time of service in return for permitting general practitioners to continue to charge their patients an additional unregulated fee.

More recently, state funding of private providers has occurred when a service previously regarded as a private responsibility has come to be seen as a full or partial public responsibility. A service may come to be seen as a 'merit good' (that is, a good people ought to consume or at least have an equitable opportunity to consume), perhaps because of a new awareness of its social benefits, such as with early childhood education. Since the 1940s, certain legal services have shifted from being entirely private matters to the state assuming responsibility for ensuring a minimum level of access for subgroups of the population to specific types of legal services. More recently, early childhood education has become another service where the scope of state responsibility and involvement as funder has increased in response to the perceived value to society of children accessing such education. In both the legal and education services, public and private finance are combined by many users.

Early childhood education in New Zealand is offered by a variety of providers (including not-for-profit and business operators) that receive government funding as well as fees and/or donations. In July 2007, the government introduced the 20 Hours Free policy for all three- and four-year-olds enrolled in teacher-led services (Ministry of Education, 2007b). Participating services cannot charge for the 20 baseline hours, but may charge for additional hours or services provided. By October 2008, 86% of eligible early childhood education services and 93% of eligible children were participating in the scheme (Bushouse, 2009). Since taking office in November 2008, the National-led government has announced that the programme will be extended from July 2010 to include five-year olds and those attending parent-led playcentres and kōhanga reo (Minister of Education (A Tolley), 2009).[3] The government has also dropped the use of the word 'free' from the policy.

The former Labour-led government's 10-year strategic plan for early childhood education, *Pathways to the Future: Ngā Huarahi Arataki* (Ministry of Education, 2002), provides background to the 20 Hours Free policy. The plan had three goals: increasing participation in quality early childhood education services (particularly for communities with low participation – Māori, Pasifika, low socioeconomic, and rural communities), improving the quality of early childhood education services, and promoting collaborative. The 20 Hours Free policy aimed to contribute to the first two of these goals. The free provision was intended to remove a cost barrier to children and families' participation, while the insistence on teacher-led services was intended to improve the quality of pre-school education. In addition, policy papers identify a further potential benefit of the policy in terms of increasing labour market participation, particularly of mothers (Office of the Minister of Education and Office of the Acting Minister for Social Development and Employment, 2004). Bushouse (2009) notes that the programme and its funding signalled two important policy changes: a shift from a subsidy to covering the full cost of services and the limitation of participation to teacher-led services, representing policy shifts to universal access to early childhood education and a greater focus on its quality. Public funding was thus being used to direct several of the government's social and economic aims through non-government providers. However, the government does not own early childhood education services, so could not require them to participate in the programme and could not regulate the supply of 20 hours' free services, and parents were not guaranteed a place for their child (Bushouse, 2008).

In determining how the policy should be funded, policy advice to the government considered several factors. It was noted that the Organisation for Economic Co-operation and Development (OECD)

---

3    Kōhanga reo is a form of early childhood designed to immerse children in Māori language and culture.

usually favours greater use of public funding channelled to parents as service users (such as vouchers), because this is considered to stimulate demand and give greater control and choice to parents (Office of the Minister of Education and Office of the Acting Minister for Social Development and Employment, 2004). However, in the then existing New Zealand system, providers were bulk funded, and a fundamental change to this was considered likely to contradict the direction of the early childhood education strategic plan and not be feasible within previously signalled timeframes (Office of the Minister of Education and Office of the Acting Minister for Social Development and Employment, 2004). Secondly, funding had to be acceptable to service providers, so they would adopt the policy.

Officials identified three tests of success for free early childhood education rates: they would fund the average cost of service provision, they would be accepted as adequate by most services, and they would not change incentives for early childhood education provision or fee levels for children not receiving free early childhood education (Le Quesne, 2006). Considerations included that many services charged similar fees for all age groups and used fees from three- to four-year-olds to subsidise the more expensive provision of services for younger children (who require more staff per child) and the need to cover property costs (a change from current policy) (Cabinet Business Committee, 2006b; Le Quesne, 2006).

The final funding rates were described as tailored (with 15 rates to reflect significant differences in the cost of operating different services), evidence-based (with information from over half the services eligible to provide free early childhood education), comprehensive (taking all costs of providing the service into account), and adequate (fully funding average costs) (Cabinet Business Committee, 2006a). Funding is also linked to each eligible child's participation in contrast to the former system that funded occupied licensed places (Ministry of Education, 2007a). Although the initial policy announced in the 2004 Budget funded only teacher-led services that were community-based (that is, not-for-profit services), the policy was extended to all teacher-led services in the 2006 Budget (Ministry of Education, 2007a).

A study for the Ministry of Education of the early implementation of the 20 Hours Free policy interviewed people involved in 60 early childhood services (chosen for diversity of types of service rather than to be statistically representative) (Froese, 2008). The key findings from the study were that:

- nearly half the services reported that their enrolment (total hours for all children) had increased since the introduction of free early childhood education (where enrolment remained the same, this was often due to the service already being full)

- more three- and four-year-old children were reported to be attending early childhood education services and attending for longer days or more days per week

- most services decided to provide free early childhood education to benefit parents, but the most important factor influencing a service's participation was the funding rate, since this had implications for the financial sustainability of the service

- by March 2008, half the services reported they were somewhat or much better off financially after free early childhood education; about 40% reported little or no change to their financial position; and just over 10% were somewhat or much worse off financially.

The Ministry of Education also surveyed a random sample of about half the playcentres in November 2007 (response rate 66%) to determine the impact of the 20 Hours Free policy on playcentres (which were not eligible to participate at the time) (Morrison, 2008). Overall, it appeared participation at playcentres had fallen, which could be attributed to the policy attracting families to alternative services, but the experience of individual playcentres varied considerably and 41% said the policy had had no impact on their service.

An article in the *Dominion Post* questioned whether the 20 Hours Free policy was achieving its aim of increasing early childhood participation, particularly by high-needs children (that is, children from Māori, Pacific, and low-income families), noting little change in participation by Māori children and significantly lower pre-school attendance by children starting at decile 1 schools compared with children starting at decile 10 schools (Catherall, 2009).[4] Officials had raised concerns about the 'deadweight cost' of the policy whereby the first beneficiaries would be parents and children already accessing and paying for services that the government would now be funding (Catherall, 2009). Officials suggested a targeted approach would bring greater benefits to those who most needed greater access (Ministry of Education, 2008). An early childhood lecturer called on the government to take a more active role in planning and providing services, especially in high-need areas, rather than relying on a market approach lest poorer communities miss out (Catherall, 2009). And while some suggested expanding the policy to include two-year-olds, others questioned the value of extending the time pre-school children could spend in out-of-home education and care (Catherall, 2009).

In July 2009, the National-led government appointed a taskforce, the 2025 Taskforce, to advise about how best to close the income gap between New Zealanders and Australians by 2025. The first report of the taskforce noted a large increase in government expenditure since about 2005 and asserted that the economic case for much of this increase was poor, citing the examples of interest-free student loans and the trebling of subsidies for early childhood education (2025 Taskforce, 2009). The report's first recommendation for education was that, 'The substantial increases in subsidies since 2005 for early childhood education and day-care should be reversed' (2025 Taskforce, 2009, p 9). However, the initial government response was to reject cutting government spending on social services.

Moving now to aged care, user charges for these services are common in the European Union, but the balance of funding for these services between the state and the individual and their family is a topic of current debate given demographic changes, equity issues, and

---

4    Decile 1 schools are the 10% of schools with the largest proportion of students from low socioeconomic communities. Decile 10 schools are the 10% of schools with the smallest proportion of students from low socioeconomic communities.

concerns that increased public funding could displace private informal care and lead to higher costs for the state (Robinson, 2004).

The funding of the long-term care of older people in England has been the subject of discussion over the last few years. In 2006, the King's Fund published a review that sought to determine how much should be spent on social care for older people over the following 20 years and what funding arrangements were needed (Wanless, 2006). The review identified several possible funding models for social care (at p xxix), including:

- some form of universal entitlement to social care that is state supported and not means-tested
- a social insurance model in which the state acts as an insurer and provides a package of care for people enrolled in the scheme should they need care
- a partnership between the state and individual where costs of care are shared for those needing care
- a limited liability model that caps an individual's liability for social care costs, whether after a certain period or after the individual has made a specified financial outlay
- a saving-based model, perhaps with a link to pension provisions, where the state contributes to an earmarked savings fund that the individual can use to pay for care.

The review used several tests to narrow down these options: fairness, economic efficiency, user choice, physical resource development, clarity, and sustainability or acceptability. The top-scoring option was the partnership model, which would provide people with a free-of-charge minimum guaranteed amount of care, above which individuals could make contributions that the state would match (up to a limit). People on low incomes would be supported through the benefits system to make additional contributions.

The review identified the strengths of the partnership model as follows (Wanless, 2006, p xxxiii). The partnership model:

- limits means-testing to the benefits system, leaving care services to focus on meeting need

- provides a guaranteed minimum level of care, making the system universal and inclusive
- provides incentives for people to save for their needs in older age as almost everyone is required to make some contribution
- produces the best value for money (that is, the best ratio of outcomes to costs)
- forces far fewer people to dispose of assets to pay for care than occurs under means-testing
- is sustainable – the system will cost more than if means-testing occurred, but it provides significant additional value by way of better outcomes and makes a charge that deters use of the service beyond the benchmark level and is an important source of revenue.

The review noted two weaknesses in the partnership model with the existing means-testing: the partnership model would not be as financially progressive and would be more expensive (by about £3.6 billion at 2004/05 prices).

The Joseph Rowntree Foundation has also been leading a programme of work on reforming the funding of long-term care. The foundation asserts the current United Kingdom system of paying for long-term care is inadequate in terms of overall funding levels, lacks coherence, and is not fair. The foundation has identified six core principles for a sustainable system of long-term care funding (Hirsch, 2005). A sustainable funding system must:

- be fair and be seen to be fair
- support preventative measures
- recognise the diversity of needs and allow recipients of care to retain their dignity
- promote personal and family responsibility
- be sustainable
- encourage an efficient supply response.

Foundation papers suggest a variety of reform options, including incremental improvements to the present funding system as well as changing to a completely different model (Hirsch, 2005, 2006; Joseph Rowntree Foundation, 2006).

In 2007, a coalition of 15 organisations from across the long-term care system, Caring Choices, held a series of discussions and undertook a survey on how care should best be funded. Most participants tended to agree that:

- the present system is not working
- more money is needed to meet growing need
- there should be a clear entitlement to some level of state-supported care regardless of income or wealth
- individuals should make a contribution to the cost of their own care, rather than expecting the state to pay for everything
- there should be strong support for unpaid carers (Caring Choices, 2008).

During 2008, the Labour government in England spent six months engaging with the public, service users, and professionals about their views on care and support issues. This engagement resulted in a Green Paper, *Shaping the Future of Care Together*, in which the government set out its vision of a high-quality, national care service that is 'fair, simple and affordable for everyone, underpinned by national rights and entitlements but personalised to individual needs' (HM Government, 2009, p 9). The five funding options suggested in the Green Paper were:

- individuals pay for themselves (which was ruled out as many people would be left without the care and support they need)
- partnership (government support of about a quarter to a third of costs – more for the less well-off – with individuals paying the remainder themselves)
- insurance (a proportion of funding provided by the state as above, with people having the option of insurance for additional costs)
- comprehensive (free care for all provided through a compulsory state insurance scheme)
- tax funded (which was ruled out because of the heavy burden it would place on working-age people).

The government's preferred option is the partnership model, because it believes this model allocates funding more fairly and many people would get all their basic care and support free. Public responses to the Green Paper were invited, and a White Paper with implementation details is to be produced in 2010.

The decision to charge service users a fee for a part publicly funded and privately provided service adds an important dimension to the policy setting. In addition to the state funding a provider to deliver public services, the recipient of the service is a co-funder of the service. There are, therefore, three key players when the state funds private providers of public services in a mixed manner: the public funder (with funding direct to the provider or through a subsidy to the user), the user as private funder (through insurance or an out-of-pocket payment) to the provider directly or the public funding agency, and the private provider (see Figure 2.1).

**Figure 2.1:** 'Mixed' public and private financing of a 'public' service

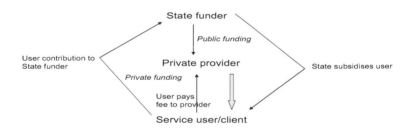

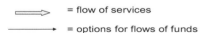  = flow of services

————▸  = options for flows of funds

Note: For simplicity, this figure excludes the role of private insurers. However, private insurers can pay providers their fees directly or reimburse their insurees for their out-of-pocket payment of fees.

A public funder's decision to use private providers to deliver public services, while including or retaining a user contribution, raises important policy questions.

- What is the objective of the policy of mixed finance? For example, is the objective to deter unnecessary consumption, contain public expenditure, contain total expenditure, raise revenue (and thereby expand public coverage), encourage population subgroups (for example, those on low incomes) to increase their use of services (by reducing their out-of-pocket payments below full price), or give users a greater stake and influence over providers (since they pay part of the cost of services directly)?

- Why, for a particular service, might a government select a particular method and balance of public and private financing, including user charging? As Robinson (2004, p 9) pointed out in his review of the European experience of mixed funding of a variety of public services:

  Charges should enable one to better secure the underlying economic, social and/or environmental objectives that the delivery of public services is ultimately geared towards.

- How will the service as a whole be priced?

- What proportion of the price of the service should the state bear compared with the proportion users bear (how big a fee or co-payment will users be charged for a service; will these fees vary by type of service or reason for using the service)?

- What effect will fee levels have on access, use, and outcomes of a service?

- How will any user fees be set and by whom (for example, by the public funder, by the provider on the basis of what the subsidised market will bear, or through a negotiation between the two)?

- On what basis will users pay fees (for example, on the basis of their income, the type of service they require, or a proportion of the cost of a service)?

- To whom should fees be paid?

- How will fees be regulated, if at all?

- How should providers be publicly reimbursed for their services or users subsidised (for example, a fee for service or a fixed subsidy irrespective of the number of services received)?
- Should the public share of finance go to the user and thence to the provider or should it go directly from the state to the provider?
- Will providers be selected for the role by the government or will users have free choice of any provider (for example, who meets minimum standards)?
- What constitutes the core service and what constitutes extras?
- What agreement or contract (if any) will be put in place between the state and providers relating to the public share of finance?
- How will private providers be incentivised to deliver public policy priorities, thereby justifying their public share of funding?
- How will the state avoid its contribution being used simply to increase incomes or reduce efficient competition within a service?
- How will probity in the use of resources and good governance in respect of the stewardship of public money be assured?
- How will service quality be assessed (for example, to inform potential users) and regulated?

In each of the service areas considered in this book, several more-specific policy issues arise from the involvement of the three key actors in the financing process (the state, the provider, and the user), and the difficulty inherent in trying to align the objectives and incentives faced by each.

For example, in the case of legal aid, the policy issues related to funding and charging include:

- how to ensure access to some minimum level of legal services for individuals who are otherwise unable to afford them
- how to develop robust methods for ensuring fair access to such services and proper assessment of people's means
- how much of a contribution to the cost of legal aid-funded services users should make, especially if access to legal aid encompasses people on middle as well as low incomes or the government

believes service users should have a direct 'customer' relationship with the provider

- how to determine the most appropriate method for remunerating lawyers who provide legal aid services, including how far the focus of remuneration should be on the hours worked by lawyers or on the quality of service delivered to clients (that is, outcomes)
- how to ensure the sector is developed so it can deliver legal services in a sustainable manner
- how to manage circumstances where costs are awarded or compensation is paid.

A key question to consider in relation to the mixed financing of public services is what effect user charges will have on the utilisation of services and therefore on the desired outcome of the service and any inequalities in the distribution of this outcome between population subgroups (for example, between poorer and wealthier people). The most important study to address this question in the health field was the RAND Health Insurance Experiment carried out in the United States in the mid-1970s. Some 2,000 non-elderly families (about 5,800 people in total) were recruited and randomly assigned to health plans with differing levels of patient co-insurance ranging from zero to 95% (Gruber, 2006). In addition, maximum out-of-pocket dollar expenditure varied from 5% to 15% up to a maximum of $1,000. Individuals were followed for up to five years.

Key lessons from the study were as follows (Gruber, 2006).

- *The co-insurance rate matters for medical utilisation and expenditure:* Higher co-insurance rates led to sizeable declines in outpatient and inpatient medical utilisation. Although 87% of people with a free care plan used care, only 68% of those with a 95% co-insurance rate used care.
- *Co-insurance effects are relatively constant across services:* Increasing co-insurance rates decreased not only the number of physician visits, but the use of all other health care services (including dental care, prescription drugs, and mental health services). The use of preventive care services was also significantly

lower, raising concern that co-insurance could save money initially, but would adversely affect health in the longer term. In addition, both care considered 'effective' and care deemed 'ineffective' were reduced by about the same amount.[5]

- *Higher co-insurance rates do not have adverse health consequences for the 'average' person:* Neither general indices of health nor the predicted risk of dying showed significant differences between the free care group and all others with co-insurance. This finding suggested that the typical enrolee was on the 'flat of the medical effectiveness curve' where additional care was not medically effective and could therefore be reduced without adverse health consequences for the average person. However, because individuals were followed for only a short time, long-term impacts were not measured, so the adverse consequences of co-insurance could be understated.

- *The poor and sick experience different effects:* For a person in average health, the differences in health care utilisation or health outcomes between rich and poor were small. However, this was in part due to out-of-pocket expenses being income-related and capped. Thus, the study understated the differences in co-payment effects between high and low income groups, although it was thought this effect might not be large. For some types of use, however, there were differential effects between rich and poor in response to co-insurance compared with free care (notably in dental care and effective care among children). Those in poor health or at risk of poor health were found to be at significantly higher risk of dying if they were on a co-insurance plan rather than a free care plan. These differences were larger for individuals with both a low income and a high risk of illness. Although not statistically significant, these findings were considered of concern.

---

5   'Effective care' is care that improves health, without regard to economic trade-offs. All other care is unnecessary or harmful (Keeler, 1995).

Advances in the effectiveness of medical care over the past 30 years may mean that care foregone because of the deterrent effect of user charges has more impact on health incomes than when the RAND experiment was carried out.

User fees have been a particular response to rising pharmaceutical expenditure. A recent systematic review looked at the effects of cost sharing on vulnerable populations (the poor and those with chronic illnesses), who would be expected to be most affected by user fees (Lexchin and Grootendorst, 2004). Cost sharing in most cases decreased prescription drug use in these groups. This in turn reduced immediate drug costs for the payer, but these savings were potentially offset by increases in other health care areas. Cost sharing led to patients foregoing essential medications with consequent increases in use of emergency services, nursing home admissions, and serious adverse events (see also Tamblyn et al, 2008).

This conclusion from the health literature is that user charges have to be employed with great care, especially because of their potential to seriously and negatively affect service use by those on lower incomes or more likely to need services. Protecting the former group may be relatively straightforward as subsidies can be targeted by income, but protecting the latter group from foregoing beneficial services is far harder to achieve through a targeted approach to funding because they may be harder to identify. As a result, the predominant view among health policy analysts is that extensive cost-sharing harms equity and may adversely affect efficiency since it appears to deter more and less effective use of services to the same extent.

This chapter has discussed some of the key frameworks and literatures relevant to our discussion of mixed financing arrangements in public services. In chapter 3, we set out how general practice, long-term care for older people, legal aid, and early childhood education are funded in New Zealand, Australia, and England. This discussion forms the basis for the typology of mixed funding approaches that is set out in chapter 4.

**3**

# Four Public Services in Three Countries

## Political context and history of services

To understand the mixed funding of public services that exists in New Zealand, Australia, and England, we need first to know something about the historical and political context in which the services have arisen. A brief background to government service provision in each of the three countries is followed by a description of the funding approach for general practice, long-term care of older people, legal aid, and early childhood education. This information is as accurate and up to date as possible, but these are rapidly changing policy areas. For example, the original New Zealand '20 Hours Free policy' is now referred to as '20 Hours ECE' (early childhood education), and the Australian 'Child Care Tax Rebate' is now the 'Child Care Rebate'. There may be other changes of which we are unaware.

### New Zealand

#### General practice

New Zealand's social welfare system substantially dates from the first Labour government and its Social Security Act 1938. This Act provided an extensive variety of taxation-funded benefits to replace a limited range of pensions ('Scope of legislation 1938', no date) The General Medical Services scheme introduced in 1941 provided a universal subsidy for general practitioner (GP) services, although GPs retained the right to charge patients ('Social security: Health benefits', no date). A mixture of public and private (patient co-payment) finance for primary care has continued since then.

#### Long-term care of older people

Care of older people began as a family responsibility, with some care provided for the 'needy' from charity. Much residential care was initially developed by non-profit providers, with some state hospital care. The sector has undergone profound change in the past 20 years, with a diminishing role for non-profit providers and a growing presence of for-profit providers in the long-term residential care sector and the growth of a varied set of providers in the home care sector (also known as community care).

Following the Health and Disability Services Act 1993, responsibility for disability support services (including aged care) moved from the Department of Social Welfare to the Ministry of Health and the then existing regional health authorities (Ashton, 2000). Subsequently district health boards continue to fund long-term residential care and some home-based care for older people who have passed a needs assessment, with means-tested contributions made by individuals for their care.

*Legal aid*

Criminal legal aid provision in New Zealand dates from the Justices of the Peace Amendment Act 1912, which allowed the Crown (at the discretion of judges) 'to assign counsel to people of insufficient means defending an indictable charge' (Saville-Smith et al, 1995, p 1). Other legislation has followed. In terms of civil legal aid, the legal profession provided some services free of charge until the Legal Aid Act 1969 made available some financial assistance for those with limited income and capital (ADLS, 1989). The present Legal Services Agency is a Crown entity set up by the Legal Services Act 2000. The agency's purpose includes providing a legal aid scheme to enable people who cannot afford legal services to access them (encompassing criminal, family and civil cases) and supporting community legal services by funding community law centres, education, and research (Legal Services Agency, no date, c). The Legal Services Amendment Act 2006 extended eligibility for legal aid, while at the same time requiring a larger proportion of recipients to repay some or all of their grant (Burton, 2006).

*Early childhood education*

Several organisations provide early childhood education in New Zealand. The Free Kindergarten movement began in Dunedin in 1889. Kindergartens received no government funding until 1909 when a capitation grant of £2 was made. The grant was based on average attendance and required an equal sum to be raised locally (New Zealand Kindergartens Inc, no date). In 1965, the government accepted responsibility for all kindergarten teachers' salaries. Since 1992, the government has bulk-funded kindergartens (New Zealand Kindergartens Inc, no date).

Playcentres, based on the ideas of child-initiated play and 'parents as first educators', began to be established in the 1930s and have received some government funding since the late 1940s (Ministry for Culture and Heritage, 2007; New Zealand Playcentre Federation, no date).

There are now many other community, private, and home-based providers of early childhood care and education, including kōhanga reo and Pacific education and care centres, which are also eligible for some government funding.

## Australia

*General practice*

In Australia, medical care has been characterised since its inception by independent medical practitioners, a fee-for-service approach to reimbursing non-hospital care, and a mixture of private and public funding. In the 19th century, public hospitals were largely charitable organisations supported by subsidies from the colonial government while private hospitals and community-based medical services charged patients on a fee-for-service basis (Healy et al, 2006). At the beginning of the 20th century, the Constitution gave the states responsibility for health care delivery. However, the Commonwealth's role in health care expanded with the challenges of the 1918 influenza epidemic, the funding of repatriation hospitals for returned service men, and the 1946 constitutional amendment of social policy, which provided a legal basis for national legislation on health care, yet restricted the Commonwealth by ensuring medical practitioners could not be forced to work for the government (no civil 'conscription') (Healy et al, 2006).

The main elements of the current system of public subsidies of private user charges for non-hospital medical care were established by the Whitlam Labor government in the Health Insurance Act 1973, which established Medibank, and in subsequent amendments that culminated in the Hawke Labor government's introduction of Medicare in 1984.

*Long-term care of older people*
Care of older people in Australia began with family care and charitable services, with limited government funds for asylums for the 'indigent' (Fine, 1999). From the 1860s to 1950, specialised nursing care developed, state governments became responsible for more asylums, and an Old Age Pension was introduced in 1901 (Fine, 1999). After World War Two, social provision of care expanded, including subsidies for nursing homes, which led to the growth of private providers (Fine, 1999). Since 1980, awareness of population ageing and increasing costs of care have seen a reorientation of policy away from institutional care towards community care (Fine, 1999).

*Legal aid*
Informal legal aid was available in 19th century Australia through 'pauper's rules' and pro bono services; the earliest statutory legal aid schemes were for people charged with criminal offences (Lynch, 2001). Public Solicitor Offices were established in South Australia (1925), Victoria (1928), and New South Wales (1943), marking the beginning of more extensive state funding (Lynch, 2001). During 1973 to 1975, the Commonwealth government established a national system called the Australian Legal Aid Office. This system was changed by the following Liberal government to give the states the responsibility for providing legal aid, with funding shared between states and Commonwealth governments (Noone, 2001). This system continues with the current independent state Legal Aid Commissions.

*Early childhood education*

The history of childcare in Australia includes the emergence of kindergartens, pre-schools, and day nurseries from 1890, with Commonwealth-funded demonstration centres and kindergartens in each state from 1940 (Fine, 1999). Since 1970, service provision has expanded, as has Commonwealth and state funding, with a shift in the 1990s from operational grants and means-tested per capita grants given to centres to the present user subsidy (Fine, 1999).

## England

*General practice*

In England, the basic organisation of primary care was determined by the National Health Service Act 1946, in which the Atlee government established state responsibility for the delivery of universal health care, free at the point of service, from 'cradle to grave'. However, the Atlee Labour government allowed GPs to remain independent contractors to the National Health Service (NHS) and a private sector in health care to exist.

Patients must enrol with a general practice to receive NHS care. Charges are levied by the NHS for prescriptions from GPs unless the patient is a member of an exempt group (for example, people aged over 65, people with certain long-term conditions, people on welfare benefits, pregnant women, children, and students). Although the balance of capitation payments, fee-for-service payments, allowances, and infrastructural funding in the GP contract with the NHS have been modified over the past 60 years, the basic contours of the financing of the GP service have altered little.

*Long-term care of older people*

The institutional framework for the provision of care for older people in England has its origins in the National Assistance Act 1948, which gave local authorities the duty to provide residential accommodation for those in need. From its inception, the care of older people has been means-tested, so not universally provided, in contrast to the NHS. Means-testing has been a recurring source of tension for users given the overlap

31

between the services. During the 1960s, 1970s, and 1980s, recognition that most care for older people should be provided in the community (that is, in people's own homes) increased, but little provision was developed. By the time of the 1988 Griffiths Report, income support benefits were being used to fund means-tested contributions for residential care. The Community Care Act 1990 made local authorities responsible for planning community care services based on an assessment of the needs of individuals and carers. Services were to respond flexibly and sensitively to need, provide a variety of options, foster independence, and concentrate on people with the greatest need. The reforms gave funding to local authorities, but also introduced new and maintained old tensions: the reforms aimed to introduce market discipline and provider competition, yet required authorities to work together; the reforms did not address the overlap between social care and health care provision, yet sought improved coordination of services.

The Royal Commission on Long-Term Care was divided in its recommendations regarding funding (Royal Commission on Long Term Care, 1999). A majority of commissioners recommended that personal care should be provided universally on the basis of need, free of charge, while a minority recommended a more generous means test. The Labour government took the latter option. In the subsequent decade, the cost implications for the NHS of gaps in social care became increasingly apparent. The means test and the concentration on those most in need led to an increase of intensive (and therefore more costly) intervention (cited in Glasby and Littlechild, 2000) and a lack of timely discharge from hospital for those excluded from social care (Glasby et al, 2006). This has led to a renewed focus on prevention and low-level support, partly through partnerships between health and social care.

*Legal aid*
Legal aid in England dates back to an Act of 1495 that introduced the *in forma pauperis* procedure, which allowed poor people to sue without having to pay court fees and assigned them a solicitor or counsel who would act charitably on their behalf (Pollock, 1975). The state's contribution to criminal legal aid dates from the Criminal Appeal Act

1907 and civil legal aid from the Legal Aid and Advice Act 1949 (Pollock, 1975). Currently, the Legal Services Commission administers legal aid under the Access to Justice Act 1999, which covers criminal and civil cases.

*Early childhood education*

Early childhood care and education in England began to develop on a voluntary and philanthropic basis in the late 18th century (Kwon, 2002). The Education Act 1870 established compulsory elementary schools for all children from the age of five, but younger children were sometimes admitted too, until this practice was officially stopped in 1905 (Kwon, 2002).

In 1923, the Nursery Schools Association was formed to improve nursery schools. Progress was slow, but by 1928, 13 publicly funded nurseries had been created and 15 other nurseries received grants. Publicly funded day nurseries expanded significantly during World War One and World War Two to enable women to work in factories. After both wars most of the nurseries were closed and funding for public nurseries became limited (Whitbread, 1972).

In the 1960s and 1970s publicly funded childcare was considered a social care service based on a parent's situation rather than a child's needs (Statham, 1997).

The 1990s saw an emphasis on quality in early childhood education. A voucher scheme was introduced in 1996 by a Conservative government for parents of four-year-olds attending early childhood services that met the government's desired curriculum framework (Kwon, 2002). The Labour government that followed in 1997 abolished the voucher scheme and directly funded pre-school services that met the requirements of a framework of early learning goals for three- and four-year-olds (Kwon, 2002).

# Funding of general practice

## *New Zealand*

General practices are independent businesses that charge fees to patients who are regarded as consumers with the right to choose and move between practices (albeit movement that is limited by GP availability, particularly in rural areas and smaller provincial centres). The quality of general practice services in New Zealand scores highly in international studies, with the main criticism being the extent to which cost can act as a barrier to access for low-income people (Schoen and Doty, 2004; Schoen et al, 2004). Since 2002, the government has sought to address this issue by providing capitation-based funding to district health boards, which then contract with primary health organisations. These, in turn, pass funding to practices so they can reduce their fees to users. Additional funding is available to practices through primary health organisations for specific initiatives such as health promotion.

The central government and district health boards have no direct contracts with general practices. In addition, no statutory system regulates the amount or percentage of costs of general medical services to be met by patients out of pocket. Instead, practices suspected of being outliers against local fee agreements between district health boards and primary health organisations can be taken through a local fee review process (Ministry of Health, 2006). Recently, the government attempted to lock in lower charges with primary health organisations through agreements to maintain low fees in return for higher subsidies; this Very Low Cost Access scheme was introduced on 1 October 2006 (Ministry of Health, 2009).

District health boards administer a national primary health organisation performance programme, which entails payments to primary health organisations (that elect to join the scheme) that achieve a core set of national performance indicators such as levels of immunisation. District health boards and private providers also directly contract selected primary care services, especially after-hours clinics (DHBNZ, no date).

The government subsidises the cost of prescription items, with the public drug-buying agency, Pharmaceutical Management Agency of New Zealand (Pharmac), determining the list of subsidised medicines. Charges are lower for scripts issued by a primary health organisation or public hospital (free for children under six years, $3 per prescription item for others) compared with $15 per item for prescriptions from a private specialist. However, GPs can and do charge for writing a prescription (the amount varies from practice to practice), and patients buy at their own expense medicines not on the Pharmac list. Individuals or families who have many prescriptions may qualify for a pharmaceutical subsidy card, which further lowers the cost of prescriptions (Ministry of Health, 2007b).

### Australia

Most Australian GPs are self-employed private practitioners working in group practices that operate as small businesses. Most practices belong to a division of general practice. These practices serve as support, education, and primary care development organisations locally. Patients are free to choose the GP they want to consult and do not need to register, although choice may be limited in rural and outlying areas (Healy et al, 2006).

Medicare is Australia's universal health care system that provides free treatment in public hospitals and free or subsidised treatment by medical practitioners, including GPs (Medicare Australia, 2009b). The Australian government sets the Medicare Benefits Schedule of charges for medical services (Medicare Australia, 2009c). GPs may 'bulk bill' Medicare for services delivered to patients or directly charge the patient, who then claims back the costs from Medicare (Healy et al, 2006). Medicare pays the full Medicare Benefits Schedule fee for GP services, but practices may also charge patients a co-payment above the level of the scheduled fee (Healy et al, 2006). Government (Medicare) funding extends to a variety of primary health care services over and above first contact GP care, 85% of the cost of which is reimbursed (Medicare Australia, 2009a). The patient pays the 15% difference plus the difference between the schedule fee and the practitioner's charge. The

15% difference is limited to a maximum amount indexed annually. Beyond this, an individual or a family may be eligible for higher Medicare benefits (referred to as the Medicare Safety Net) (Medicare Australia, 2010).

The system is partly funded by a Medicare levy of 1.5% of taxable income, with the balance of public funding coming from general taxation (Healy et al, 2006). Low-income earners, among others, are exempt from the levy, and people on high incomes who do not have private hospital insurance pay a higher rate or surcharge (an additional 1%). Private health insurance does not cover primary care; substantial tax incentives are offered to encourage users to purchase private medical insurance (Healy et al, 2006).

The Pharmaceutical Benefits Scheme subsidises the purchase of most prescription medicines. (From 1 January 2009, a prescription cost up to $32.90 for most users or $5.30 for people qualified for a concession card. The Australian government picks up the remaining cost of a generic drug. These figures are indexed to inflation on an annual basis (Australian Government DHA, 2010a). Above a certain annual threshold of expenditure, ordinary users qualify for the concessionary rate and concession card holders receive free prescriptions (Australian Government DHA, 2010b).

*England*

The public in England has the right to receive comprehensive primary care services that are free at the point of delivery through the NHS. People must be registered with a single practice, although they can access NHS GP services from other practices when they are away from home. Other recent developments in first contact care have enabled patients to seek GP and nurse care outside their registered practice from, for example, NHS walk-in centres in convenient town centre locations and on hospital sites. The state provides funding through primary care trusts, which contract with general practices on a mixed capitation and pay-for-performance basis to provide core general practice and discretionary additional or enhanced services. Infrastructure payments are also included in the national contract. The government has encouraged primary care trusts to use tendering and competition to improve access to, and the responsiveness of, NHS primary care services (Ellins et al, 2008).

Practices operate as independent businesses, albeit without the right to charge their NHS-enrolled patients (they can have fully private patients) and receive almost all of their funding through their contracts with the primary care trust. This contract is nationally negotiated and locally implemented and includes performance indicators with associated payments.

The NHS sets prescription fees. From 1 April 2009, a standard prescription cost £7.20 per item (UK Department of Health, 2009). However, prescriptions are free for people aged under 16, people aged under 18 and in full-time education, people aged over 60, hospital inpatients, and people with various medical diagnoses or entitlements (for example, on income support or with low incomes) (NHS, 2009).

## Funding of long-term care of older people

### *New Zealand*

The Ministry of Health funds district health boards to contract for disability support (social care) services in people's own homes, rest homes (residential care), and hospitals. Users are needs-assessed, then asset-tested to determine their eligibility for a state subsidy towards the cost of rest home care (Ministry of Health, 2007a). The individual's contribution towards costs involves a charge on their state superannuation (pension) plus a contribution determined through an income test. The residential care subsidy, paid directly to the provider by the district health board, is set at a level that pays the balance of the contracted cost of care that is not covered by the individual's contribution. Individuals who have been assessed as requiring long-term residential care, but who do not qualify for the residential care subsidy because of the assets and income tests, may qualify for a residential care loan whereby the state advances money directly to a provider for the payment of long-term residential care, with the money secured against the individual's home (Ministry of Health, 2007a; Work and Income, no date).

District health boards contract with private and non-governmental organisation providers and may also directly provide some services. Providers are subject to a national price schedule for contracts negotiated with district health boards in addition to the co-payments some users make after means-testing. Providers are subject to government regulation, quality specifications, and audit (Ministry of Health, 2008b). Users and their carers have relatively few choices of model of care with a predominant reliance on institutional care in rest homes, although there are moves to develop more home-based intensive support.

Home-based support services are funded by the Ministry of Health, which gives money to district health boards on a capitation basis. However, the rates district health boards pay to home care providers vary from district to district. Access to these services is also through a needs assessment – some services are provided free and some involve a charge to users. There is no explicit certification standard in the home care sector, although the New Zealand Home Health Association encourages its members to become voluntarily certified. Home care providers are subject to audit by district health boards.

### *Australia*

In Australia, the Commonwealth Department of Health and Ageing partly funds aged care services. Residential care for older people is hostel-based (sheltered or warden-aided housing) or nursing home-based, with people being assessed as having 'low' or 'high' needs. This assessment is made by Aged Care Assessment Teams that work according to an 'ageing in place' philosophy. Hostel care requires users to pay an asset-based bond plus a basic daily fee (nationally set), an income-tested daily fee (nationally set), and additional fees for extra services (set by the provider for a higher standard of accommodation and services) (Australian Government DHA, 2010c). Accommodation bonds are negotiated between the user and the aged care provider. No bond can be charged that would leave a person with less than $36,000 in assets. The aged care provider is allowed to retain a monthly amount from the bond (up to a nationally set maximum) for up to five years; the remainder of the bond is repaid to the person or their estate when they leave the aged care home (Australian Government DHA, 2010c). Nursing home care does not require an asset-bond, but entails an asset-based daily rate to be paid by the user (Australian Government DHA, 2010c). Providers of both forms of care are a mix of for-profit, religious, and community-based non-governmental organisations. Providers must meet the requirements of the Aged Care Act 1997. A national accreditation programme is in place, and service providers that do not meet the standards may be subject to sanctions (Aged Care Standards, no date; Australian Government DHA, 2007).

Two levels of home-based care are available for a person who wishes to be supported at home (that is, in community care). People the Aged Care Assessment Teams assesses as requiring low-level care receive a Community Aged Care Package, which is an individually tailored set of services (Australian Government DHA, 2009a). People with high needs may be eligible for the Extended Aged Care at Home programme that involves a more extensive but still flexible variety of services, including nursing, domestic assistance, personal care, transport, and social support (Australian Government DHA, 2009c). The government caps maximum daily contributions from the individual for both levels of care at $7.69 per day (as at September 2009) for those on a basic pension or, for those with other income, the maximum fee is 17.5% of income to the level of the basic pension plus up to 50% of income above that level (Australian Government DHA, 2009b). In the case of the Extended Aged Care at Home programme, the government and the provider sign a contract that sets out payment terms, standards, and service requirements for the individual (Australian Government DHA, 2009c).

## England

In England, local government funds home-based and residential social care (disability support) services, on an assets- and means-tested basis, and according to locally set eligibility criteria (UK Department of

Health, no date). Therefore, some users pay a contribution towards care costs, based on a nationally determined asset and income means test. Local authorities set their own limits in relation to what they fund as a weekly rate for residential care, so the amount a person pays, even after assessment, will vary by locality. The local authority typically contracts with a variety of providers, mainly private, but some non-governmental organisations and public providers. The NHS funds nursing care and hospital care free of charge to patients.

In theory, users and their carers have a choice of provider, but in practice they often face few choices due to hospitals being under pressure to discharge people and age care providers having a lack of capacity. Some local authorities and NHS primary care trusts have set up joint funding and planning mechanisms to enable new models of care that are less focused on residential settings.

The Care Quality Commission regulates health and social services in England provided by the NHS, private companies, or voluntary organisations (Care Quality Commission, no date). Services must be registered with the commission and demonstrate that they meet essential quality standards. One of the commission's roles is to ensure providers continue to meet standards through a variety of monitoring mechanisms. When services fail to meet standards, the commission can impose various consequences, including closing the service. The commission also aims to promote improvement and the provision of services beyond the essential standards.

## Funding of legal aid

### New Zealand

In New Zealand, the state funds legal aid through the Legal Services Agency. The agency runs a duty solicitor scheme, police detention legal assistance service, and legal information service and funds community legal services, mostly through community law centres (Legal Services Agency, no date, b). Funding is also allocated to lawyers in private practices for civil legal aid[6] and criminal legal aid services to people otherwise unable to pay for such services. For civil cases, the client approaches a lawyer who advertises that they provide legal aid services. The lawyer then applies for legal aid on the client's behalf. In criminal cases, the client may approach a lawyer of their choice or be assigned one by the agency. From 2004, a Public Defence Service was piloted with provision it take up to 33% of cases for the Auckland and Manukau courts. This scheme was made permanent in 2008 and is being extended across the Auckland region in 2009–2010.

Only specified legal services are included in the scheme, and user eligibility is determined though an income and assets test and an assessment of the seriousness of the legal issue (Legal Services Agency, no date, a). For service users above an income and asset threshold, legal aid is generally regarded as a loan with an expectation of repayment of part (or all) of the loan to the Legal Services Agency. Below this threshold, legal aid is free for clients, although they may be required to repay some or all of the aid received if money or property is recovered as a result of their case (Legal Services Agency, no date, a). Lawyers who provide legal aid services bill the agency on a case-by-case basis. Payment is made on an hourly basis, according to nationally determined rates. These rates vary according to the experience of the lawyer and the complexity of the case, but there is no formal funding cap per case. No charge is made directly to the client by the lawyer when a case is covered by legal aid. The agency runs a system for checking legal aid claims and payments to practices.

In April 2009, the Minister of Justice announced a fundamental review of the legal aid system to be led by Dame Margaret Bazley. The subsequent public discussion paper noted that demand for legal aid had been increasing (the total number of grants increased 23% between 2003 and 2008) (Legal Aid Review, 2009a). However, as government revenue was declining, increasing government funding to match increased

---

6    Civil legal aid includes Waitangi Tribunal claims cases and employment, family, refugee, and accident compensation cases.

service demand was not sustainable. The review suggested (at p 22) better ways to manage funding for legal representation to:

- ensure funding delivers quality, appropriate representation that is targeted at meeting legally aided people's needs and representing them appropriately in the justice system
- refocus the system as a whole to better enable it to meet legal needs in a way that solves people's problems and reduces further demand on the justice system
- deliver legal aid in a way that is consistent with the requirements of the justice system
- be efficient in the legal aid system's use of public funding.

The review considered seven issues for managing taxpayer funds effectively (Legal Aid Review, 2009a, p 63):

- identifying the pros and cons of capping legal aid expenditure
- addressing the key drivers of legal aid expenditure (criminal cases and administration costs)
- assessing funding models (that is, determining whether there might be efficiencies from moving away from a 'fee for hours of service' model to another model, such as bulk funding)
- putting more emphasis on mixed public–private service provision (the Public Defence Service pilot showed that, given the right conditions, a public service model could deliver legal aid services effectively and efficiently)
- reducing complexity and prescription in the legal aid system
- removing inefficient practices
- managing high-cost cases better.

Following a brief period for submissions on the discussion document, the Legal Aid Review released its findings (Legal Aid Review, 2009b). The review considered a role exists for a mixture of publicly and privately provided legal aid services. It recommended continuing the Public Defence Service in Auckland and extending the service to Wellington and Christchurch where case volumes are sufficient to make it an efficient option. The review also suggested using a Public Defence Service in smaller centres to address problems with the quality of legal aid services, and that the government should consider expanding the service to cover civil and family law cases, in addition to the current criminal law cases. In addition, the review recommended changing the Legal Services Act 2000 to enable flexibility in the procurement of services, 'using the most appropriate funding model in the proportions that will enable the best value for taxpayers' money' (Legal Aid Review, 2009b, p 100). Specifically, the review, to ensure value for money and address quality issues, proposed the bulk funding of lawyers for the delivery of a set of contracted services. The review suggested capitation, where there is a defined population and a reasonably stable and predictable cost of services per person, as another possible funding option. The government is yet to announce its decisions on the review's recommendations.

### *Australia*

Australia has eight independent Legal Aid Commissions, one in each state and territory. The Commonwealth provides funding exclusively for matters arising under Commonwealth law, and states provide legal aid funding for a variety of legal services for their populations (Victoria Legal Aid, 2007). The client approaches the local Legal Aid Commission, seeking support for legal costs. If successful, the client is allocated a lawyer to handle the case and the Legal Aid Commission pays legal aid directly to the lawyer. Legal representation through legal aid is not free – the public contribution is subject to a means test, an asset test, and an assessment of the merits of the case (Victoria Legal Aid, 2007). Successful applicants may be required to repay some or all of the costs of representation, and in some states the system is referred to as a 'grant of legal assistance'. The Legal Aid Commission may recoup costs awarded under legal aid – thus the payment in some cases may take the form of a loan.

Following a successful application for legal aid, the Legal Aid Commission appoints a salaried lawyer or a private practitioner as deemed appropriate. The mixed model is considered useful, especially when considering the rural and remote nature of much of Australia. Rates for legal aid work are usually lower than those charged in private practice and there is federal concern about lawyers pulling out of legal aid work.

### England

In England, funding is provided by the state through the Legal Services Commission to law firms to deliver legal services to clients unable to pay their own costs. Firms have to go through a national quality accreditation process to become a legal aid provider, and the legal aid scheme includes both civil and criminal matters. In civil cases, clients consult a solicitor who can apply for legal aid, which has different levels from advice to legal representation. A regional office of the Legal Services Commission assesses eligibility, which depends on the type of legal problem, results of a means test, and whether there is a reasonable chance of winning the case (Legal Services Commission, 2007c). Even if granted legal aid, a client may still have to pay some of the costs, depending on their financial situation, or repay some costs if money or property is recovered through the case (Legal Services Commission, 2007a).

The three possible levels of legal aid service in criminal cases are advice and assistance, advocacy assistance, and representation. A solicitor can determine eligibility for advice and assistance (based on financial criteria) and advocacy assistance (through a merits test and, in some cases, a financial test). Clients are not asked to pay a contribution for either of these services (Legal Services Commission, 2007b). Eligibility for legal aid for court representation is determined by the court, based on a means test and an 'interests of justice' test. If legal aid is granted, the judge, at the end of the case, may ask the client to pay a contribution if this is considered reasonable (Legal Services Commission, 2007b). Most criminal legal aid is delivered by private firms under a general criminal contract, but a four-year Public Defender Service pilot was established in 2001 and has continued on a small scale in England and Wales (Regan, 2007).

The Legal Services Commission operates a cost-per-case system for legal aid where the solicitor charges each case to the Legal Services Commission, which pays for work done in relation to the time spent on the case. However, the government has published several papers since 2005 and consulted on reform proposals that aim to move criminal legal aid to best value tendering and civil legal aid to fixed fees under a unified contract (Department for Constitutional Affairs, 2005, 2006; Department for Constitutional Affairs and Legal Services Commission, 2006). This new system will focus on the delivery of a quality service to the client that is cost-efficient for the Legal Services Commission, rather than paying for the hours a practitioner works. The proposals have been contentious with providers and slower to implement than initially planned. The government recently announced best value tendering would go ahead in two areas from October 2009, but wider implementation would be delayed until at least 2013 to enable a full evaluation of pilot schemes (UK Parliament, 2009).

## Funding of early childhood education[7]

### *New Zealand*

Since July 2007, the New Zealand Ministry of Education has paid for 20 hours per week of free early childhood education to all three- and four-year-olds enrolled in teacher-led early childhood services[8] (Ministry of Education, 2007b). This is not means tested. Providers may charge for hours beyond the 20 hours, but must keep records of this. Providers may also seek donations and charge optional fees for 'over and above' services within the free 20 hours (Ministry of Education, 2007b). Kindergartens and other community-based providers with charitable status fund raise from individuals and businesses in the community, receive grants from local government, and rely on donations from parents.

---

7    Definitions of 'early years education' and 'childcare provision' vary across countries, so caution needs to be exercised when comparing service provision and funding in this area.

8    From July 2010, this will be expanded to include five-year-olds (see Minister of Education (A Tolley), 2009; Smith, 2009).

The 20 Hours funding comes on top of base funding from the Ministry of Education. Base funding is a subsidy paid to providers according to the number of licensed places they offer. The provider claims the funding from the state on behalf of the child and carer. Work and Income New Zealand separately subsidises childcare for parents in paid work who have children aged up to 13 or children aged up to 18 if they receive the child disability allowance (up to 30 hours a week beyond the 20 free hours), and up to nine hours of childcare if the parent is not in paid work and not accessing the 20 free hours (Work and Income, 2008). The subsidies are paid directly to the service provider.

New Zealand has a tradition of a variety of childcare provision, with about half in the community-owned and non-governmental organisation sector and about half in the corporate sector. The arrival of 20 hours of free early childhood education in 2007 has seen an increasing focus on teacher-led provision, with parent-led playcentres and kōhanga reo initially excluded from eligibility for the new funding. However, the new National-led government agreed to include these services from July 2010 (Minister of Education (A Tolley), 2009). The 20 Hours policy is tightly linked to staffing and quality requirements. Additional oversight is provided through Education Review Office reviews every three years.

### Australia

The Australian government provides a means- and work hours-tested child care benefit to families with a child in government-approved care (for which opening hours, staff training, health and safety, and other quality issues are regulated) (Australian Government DEEWR, no date). A lower level of subsidy is available to help parents pay for 'registered' care, which includes relatives, nannies, and private pre-schools. The amount of subsidy is determined by family income (at a reducing rate, down to zero, with increasing income) and, for 24–50 hours' childcare per week, evidence that the parent or parents are in paid work, training, or study. The child care benefit for 'approved' care is paid directly to the childcare service or parents pay full fees and claim back an annual lump sum from the Family Assistance Office. 'Registered' care must first be paid for by parents, who then submit a claim to the Family Assistance Office.

There was also a Child Care Tax Rebate for people in the workforce. This rebate covered 50% of out-of-pocket costs for approved childcare (registered care was excluded) and was worth up to $7,500 (indexed) per child per year (Australian Government DEEWR, no date, a). Parents had to meet the paid work, training, and study tests for this rebate, but there was no income test. On 1 July 2009, the Child Care Tax Rebate was re-named the Child Care Rebate to reflect that it is no longer a tax offset under taxation legislation. The Family Assistance Office now pays the rebate to families under the family assistance law (Australian Government DEEWR, no date, b). Eligibility and entitlements have not changed.

Other government assistance with childcare costs includes a childcare benefit for grandparents who are the primary carers, extra help for parents on income support (JET – jobs, education and training – childcare fee assistance), assistance for children at risk of abuse or serious hardship, and free childcare for new migrants while they attend English language programmes (Australian Government DEEWR, no date).

### England

In England, state funding of early childhood education is mainly through the provision of a tax credit to working parents. The tax credit includes an element identified for childcare of up to 80% of the costs of approved childcare, with a maximum payment of £140 per week for one child or £240 per week for two or more children (Citizens Advice Bureau, 2010). A lone parent or two parents must be working 16 hours or more a week to qualify for the tax credit. The tax credit abates above a certain income threshold, with the childcare element of the credit being the last to be reduced (Citizens Advice Bureau, 2010).

For all children aged three and over, a nursery education grant is available either in the form of a free part-time place in a local authority–run nursery or a subsidised place in a private nursery that is accredited by the Office for Standards in Education. Payment is made directly to the provider, and parents need to pay for any time their child is at a nursery beyond the time covered by the grant. Most childcare providers are in the private sector, being nurseries run as businesses or sole-trading childminders. The Office for Standards in Education regulates childcare providers with childminders also regulated by the local authority. Many infant schools have state-run nurseries attached to them providing one year of early years education before the child starts school.

Some employers offer subsidised childcare services or childcare voucher schemes to their employees. In these schemes, the employer pays the registered child care provider directly. Employees do not pay income tax or national insurance contributions on the support, and employers do not pay national insurance contributions on the support. The exemption is provided in addition to a person's salary or through a salary sacrifice (Daycare Trust, 2010). Some local authorities also subsidise services for parents on low incomes or students. Other funding may be available for students with childcare costs through their training provider.

## Summary

The variety of financing schemes for the four public services and the complexity of some of the financing arrangements is striking. Major differences exist between schemes in which 'mixed' financing applies to the entire service and all users (for example, New Zealand general practice where all adults receive public funding and make out-of-pocket payments) compared with schemes in which specific user subgroups receive part-public funding while the rest receive no public funding (for example, English civil legal aid). A third type of scheme has specific parts of the service fully publicly funded and others requiring mixed funding (for example, New Zealand's free 20 hours of early childhood education compared with provision over 20 hours per week).

In the next chapter, a typology of approaches to mixed financing of public services is proposed, drawing on analysis of the complex and varied arrangements set out above.

# 4

## Typology of Approaches to Mixed Financing of Public Services

It is easy to become disoriented by the detail of each service in each country. Therefore, it is helpful to capture the key features of each service in each country, so inter-country comparisons can be made more easily. This is the purpose of the typology that follows.

Terms used in the typology are defined in Table 4.1. Table 4.2 sets out the generic typology, and Tables 4.3–4.6 focus on a particular service in each of the three countries.

The typology includes in each column, the arrangements for funding services, along a continuum from full government subsidy with private providers to full funding with public providers.

The typology includes in rows, the key levers or features that apply to each of the arrangements set out in the columns. These include client coverage (whether universal or targeted); the proportion of funding that is public (full or partial); the ability to charge users (yes or no); whether there is user fee regulation or not; who receives the public funding initially (the user or the provider); the payment method (fee for service, capitation, budget or mixed); the nature of the implied contract (complete – all likely issues relating to the contract are in the contract, or incomplete – not all issues are covered (Croxson et al, 2009); and an example. Not all options within each lever or feature are possible with each of the arrangements and they are left out of the table where this is the case.

Tables 4.3–4.6 highlight the substantial differences between the three countries in how they approach the mixed financing of each service. In the case of general practice, Australia and New Zealand have strong similarities, and differ markedly from England.

In the case of long-term care of older people, Australia and England show similarities with partial public subsidies of private providers while

New Zealand contracts for services from private providers though like Australia and England, only partially funds from public sources.

In the case of legal aid, each country has a range of approaches but all three systems are appreciably different.

Where early childhood education is concerned, New Zealand has gone further than either of the other two countries towards a universal service with its policy of up to 20 hours of free provision, while Australia and England have similar targeted, partially publicly financed approaches.

**Table 4.1:** Definitions of terms used in the typology

| Term | Definition |
|------|-----------|
| Grant or voucher | A means-tested grant may be made by the state to a provider to enable an individual to access a service. Alternatively, users may be given cash or vouchers to purchase services from providers of their own choice for a defined service. |
| Loans | Payment by the state of a full or partial-cost loan (repayable) to an individual to access a service). |
| Public payment modality | |
| Fee-for-service | Payment per service delivered |
| Capitation | Overall payment for a particular population or group on a per head basis, regardless of the number of individual services they utilise. The payment may be adjusted for relative needs of sub-groups. |
| Budget | An agreed total amount of funding from which all services must be provided. |
| Mixed | Some combination of fee-for-service, capitation, and budget. |
| Subsidy | A subsidy by the state of user fees. The subsidy may be full (covering the whole fee) or partial, and available universally or only for targeted groups. |
| Tax subsidy or support | Provision of a tax credit or rebate to reduce costs faced by users of a service. |

The typology of mixed financing approaches, when applied to four different public services in New Zealand, Australia, and England, reveals an interesting and complex picture. There are substantial differences both in the way each country approaches the financing arrangements for a particular public service and in how a specific country approaches the financing of different services across the public sector. For example, in New Zealand and Australia general practice is in the category of partial public subsidies with some user co-payment, but England provides full public funding through a process of contracting with providers; early childhood education in New Zealand receives a full public subsidy (for the first 20 hours per child), while Australia and England use the tax system to provide financial relief to parents. English general practice is provided on a national and publicly funded basis, but long-term care for older people is financed through a partial public subsidy along with user co-payments that local authorities determine at a local level.

These differences suggest it is inappropriate to approach the issue of mixed financing of public services from a purely international comparative approach – there is clearly no such thing as a 'typical' New Zealand, Australian, or English approach, albeit specific constitutional, cultural, and historical factors inevitably have had an influence (for example, the federal system in Australia).

Our review of the four service areas in three countries demonstrates that in each case a mix of factors has influenced the choice of financing approach. These factors include historical and contextual issues such as the relationship between a profession and government; the strength or otherwise of local compared with state or national government; and the intention behind a government's decision to partly fund a public service (for example, to stimulate demand by providing financial support, to curb demand by having the service user pay some of the cost, to influence the service model or quality, or to extend service coverage to specific population groups).

**Table 4.2:** Generic typology of approaches to mixed financing of public services

| Lever/other feature | Full subsidy, private providers | Partial subsidy, private providers | Grant/ voucher, private providers | Loans, private providers | Tax/benefits system (credits and deductions) | Full funding, public providers* |
|---|---|---|---|---|---|---|
| Client coverage | Universal<br>Targeted | Universal<br>Targeted | Universal<br>Targeted | Universal<br>Targeted | Universal<br>Targeted | Universal<br>Targeted |
| Public funding proportion | Full | Partial | Full<br>Partial | Full<br>Partial | Full<br>Partial | Full |
| Ability to charge users | No | Yes | Yes<br>No | Yes | Yes | No |
| User fee regulation | N/A | Yes<br>No | Yes<br>No | Yes<br>No | Yes<br>No | N/A |
| Recipient of public funding | User<br>Provider | User<br>Provider | User<br>Provider | User<br>Provider | User | Provider |
| Public payment modality | Fee-for-service<br>Capitation<br>Budget<br>Mixed | Fee-for-service<br>Capitation<br>Budget<br>Mixed | Fee-for-service<br>Capitation<br>Budget<br>Mixed | Budget | Budget | Fee-for-service<br>Capitation<br>Budget<br>Mixed |
| Nature of implied contract | Complete<br>Incomplete | Complete<br>Incomplete | Complete<br>Incomplete | Complete<br>Incomplete | Incomplete | Complete |

| Lever/other feature | Full subsidy, private providers | Partial subsidy, private providers | Grant/ voucher, private providers | Loans, private providers | Tax/benefits system (credits and deductions) | Full funding, public providers* |
|---|---|---|---|---|---|---|
| Examples | Criminal legal aid in England<br><br>Early years education 20 hours in NZ<br><br>General practice in England<br><br>General practice in Australia (bulk billing) | General practice in NZ<br><br>General practice in Australia (non-bulk billing)<br><br>Long-term care in NZ, Australia, and England | Children's and older people's optometry in England<br><br>Legal aid in NZ | Legal aid in Australia (some states) | Early years education in England and Australia | Public hospital system in NZ and England |

\* Outside the scope of this book, but included to complete the continuum of financing options.

**Table 4.3:** Typology of approaches to mixed financing – general practice in New Zealand, Australia, and England

| Lever/other feature | Full subsidy, private providers | Partial subsidy, private providers | Grant/voucher, private providers | Loans, private providers | Tax/benefits system (credits and deductions) |
|---|---|---|---|---|---|
| Client coverage | | | | | |
| Universal | Australia (bulk billing); England | NZ (primary health organisations; Australia (non–bulk billing) | | | |
| Targeted | | | | | |
| Public funding proportion | | | | | |
| Full | Australia (bulk billing); England | | | | |
| Partial | | NZ; Australia (non–bulk billing) | | | |
| Ability to charge users | | | | | |
| Yes | | NZ; Australia (non–bulk billing) | | | |
| No | Australia (bulk billing); England | | | | |
| User fee regulation | | | | | |
| Yes | Australia (bulk billing) | NZ (partial) | | | |
| No | | Australia | | | |
| N/A | England | | | | |

| Lever/other feature | Full subsidy, private providers | Partial subsidy, private providers | Grant/voucher, private providers | Loans, private providers | Tax/benefits system (credits and deductions) |
|---|---|---|---|---|---|
| Recipient of public funding | | | | | |
| User | | Australia (non–bulk billing) | | | |
| Provider | Australia (bulk billing); England | NZ | | | |
| Public payment modality | | | | | |
| Fee-for-service | Australia (bulk billing) | Australia (non–bulk billing) | | | |
| Capitation | | | | | |
| Budget | | | | | |
| Mixed | England | NZ (mostly capitation with some fee-for-service) | | | |
| Nature of implied contract | | | | | |
| Complete | Australia (bulk billing); England | | | | |
| Incomplete | | NZ; Australia (non–bulk billing) | | | |

**Table 4.4:** Typology of approaches to mixed financing – long-term care of older people in New Zealand, Australia, and England

| Lever/other feature | Full subsidy, private providers | Partial subsidy, private providers | Grant/voucher, private providers | Loans, private providers | Tax/benefits system (credits and deductions) |
|---|---|---|---|---|---|
| Client coverage | | | | | |
| Universal | | | | | |
| Targeted | | NZ, Australia, England | | | |
| Public funding proportion | | | | | |
| Full | | | | | |
| Partial | | NZ, Australia, England | | | |
| Ability to charge users | | | | | |
| Yes | | NZ, Australia, England | | | |
| No | | | | | |
| User fee regulation | | | | | |
| Yes | | NZ, Australia | | | |
| No | | England | | | |
| Recipient of public funding | | | | | |
| User | | | | | |
| Provider | | NZ, Australia, England | | | |

| Lever/other feature | Full subsidy, private providers | Partial subsidy, private providers | Grant/voucher, private providers | Loans, private providers | Tax/benefits system (credits and deductions) |
|---|---|---|---|---|---|
| Public payment modality | | | | | |
| Fee-for-service | | NZ, Australia, England | | | |
| Capitation | | | | | |
| Budget | | | | | |
| Mixed | | | | | |
| Nature of implied contract | | | | | |
| Complete | | NZ, England | | | |
| Incomplete | | Australia | | | |

**Table 4.5:** Typology of approaches to mixed financing – legal aid services in New Zealand, Australia, and England

| Lever/other feature | Full subsidy, private providers | Partial subsidy, private providers | Grant/voucher, private providers | Loans, private providers | Tax/benefits system (credits and deductions) |
|---|---|---|---|---|---|
| Client coverage | | | | | |
| Universal | | | | | |
| Targeted | England (criminal) | | | NZ; Australia; England (civil) | |
| Public funding proportion | | | | | |
| Full | England | | | Full or partial: NZ; England | |
| Partial | | | | Australia | |
| Ability to charge users | | | | | |
| Yes | England (judge may set a contribution if this is considered reasonable) | | | NZ (may be required to repay some or all); Australia; England | |
| No | | | | | |
| User fee regulation | | | | | |
| Yes | | | | | |
| No | | | | | |
| N/A | England | | | NZ; Australia; England | |

| Lever/other feature | Full subsidy, private providers | Partial subsidy, private providers | Grant/voucher, private providers | Loans, private providers | Tax/benefits system (credits and deductions) |
|---|---|---|---|---|---|
| Recipient of public funding | | | | | |
| User | | | | | |
| Provider | England | | | NZ; Australia; England | |
| Public payment modality | | | | | |
| Fee-for-service | England: moving to best value tendering | | | NZ; Australia; England: moving to fixed fees | |
| Capitation | | | | | |
| Budget | | | | | |
| Mixed | | | | | |
| Nature of implied contract | | | | | |
| Complete | England | | | NZ; Australia; England | |
| Incomplete | | | | | |

**Table 4.6:** Typology of approaches to mixed financing – early childhood education in New Zealand, Australia, and England

| Lever/other feature | Full subsidy, private providers | Partial subsidy, private providers | Grant/voucher, private providers | Loans, private providers | Tax/benefits system (credits and deductions) |
|---|---|---|---|---|---|
| **Client coverage** | | | | | |
| Universal | NZ | England (nursery education grant) | | | |
| Targeted | | Australia (child care benefit) | | | Australia (child care rebate); England (tax credits) |
| **Public funding proportion** | | | | | |
| Full | NZ | England (local authority (LA)–run nursery) | | | |
| Partial | | Australia; England (private nursery) | | | Australia; England |
| **Ability to charge users** | | | | | |
| Yes | | Australia; England (private) | | | Australia; England |
| No | NZ | England (LA) | | | |
| **User fee regulation** | | | | | |
| Yes | | | | | |
| No | | Australia; England (private) | | | Australia; England |
| N/A | NZ | England (LA) | | | |

| Lever/other feature | Full subsidy, private providers | Partial subsidy, private providers | Grant/voucher, private providers | Loans, private providers | Tax/benefits system (credits and deductions) |
|---|---|---|---|---|---|
| Recipient of public funding | | | | | |
| User | | Australia: user or provider / England | | | Australia; England |
| Provider | NZ | | | | |
| Public payment modality | | | | | |
| Fee-for-service | NZ | Australia; England | | | Australia; England |
| Capitation | | | | | |
| Budget | | | | | |
| Mixed | | | | | |
| Nature of implied contract | | | | | |
| Complete | | | | | |
| Incomplete | NZ | Australia; England | | | Australia; England |
| N/A | | | | | |

In the next chapter, we use the factors identified as influencing the choice of a specific approach to mixed financing to propose a framework by which one might assess the likely consequences of choosing a particular mixed funding approach for a public service.

# 5

## Criteria for Assessing Mixed Financing Approaches in Public Services

### Introduction

In earlier chapters, we described the different approaches to mixed financing of four public services in New Zealand, Australia, and England. This descriptive material was then summarised for ease of comparison in a typology of potential approaches to mixed financing of public services. The seven approaches were examined in relation to economic levers such as ability to charge users, the nature of implied contract, and the proportion of public (compared with private) funding.

In the project workshop in April 2008, participants encouraged the research team to develop a framework that could be used to assess different approaches to mixed financing of public services. In this chapter, we develop the analysis set out in the typology and suggest such a framework.

The framework sets out potential assessment criteria from the three perspectives of the state, providers, and users. The criteria have been developed based on the review of literature, semi-structured interviews with policy and provider stakeholders in the four public service areas in New Zealand, and commentary provided by participants at the project workshop.

Each assessment criterion is examined using examples drawn from the four public policy areas across the three countries. The analysis is not intended to be exhaustive, rather to demonstrate a practical way in which approaches to mixed financing might be assessed, using the three different 'lenses' of the state, providers, and users.

In chapter 6, we apply this assessment framework to general practice in the three countries.

For each criterion, tests can be applied to assess how far a particular mixed financing approach fulfils the requirements of the state, providers, and users in relation to the issue addressed by that criterion. The criteria are summarised in Table 5.7 (on pp 87–90).

## State perspective

The state considers many issues when deciding whether to provide public funding to support a particular service, and, if so, how much funding should be allocated, to whom, and on what basis. These issues include, in no order of importance:

- fiscal costs
- coverage and access to services
- degree of choice and competition
- sustaining or developing a viable market
- ability to shape services
- assurance of quality of services
- control of entry to the market
- behavioural effects of user charges
- cost shifting
- efficiency
- equity
- accountability for the use of public funds.

We consider each of these issues briefly below. By way of introduction, however, it is worth observing that mixed finance regimes of a broadly similar nature, for various reasons, may operate differently in different jurisdictions and over time. The reasons for these differences include differences in political culture, the size and structure of the economy, the pattern of provision, and the behavioural responses of users. Policy makers, therefore, need to be wary of assuming that it is possible to transplant a policy regime from one jurisdiction to another and produce identical effects.

## Fiscal costs

A decision to allocate government funding to the provision of a particular service to citizens obviously entails fiscal costs. The magnitude of these costs depends, among other things, on the nature and cost of the service, the level of the state subsidy, the eligibility criteria, and the take-up rate among the eligible population. If the service is already fully subsidised by the state, then a move to mixed financing will, with all other things staying the same, deliver fiscal savings – with the magnitude of such savings being dependent on the level of co-payments (or part charges) and any behavioural responses by providers and users. By contrast, if the service has previously been solely funded from private sources, then a shift to mixed financing will necessarily impose additional costs on the state. The same is true, of course, if a mixed financing arrangement is in place and the state decides to increase the level of public subsidies or extend the range of users who are eligible – as occurred under the recent Labour-led government in New Zealand in the areas of primary health care and early childhood education.

When the state wishes to part fund a new service, part fund a service that was previously funded solely by the private sector, or increase a subsidy being provided for a partially funded service, it needs to consider the likely magnitude of the additional fiscal costs, whether these additional costs are justified and affordable on a long-term basis, whether the new subsidy regime will be indexed (and, if so, to which index of inflation), and how the new subsidies will be financed (for example, through extra taxes or savings in other areas).

In the three countries under examination, governments have often implemented new or more generous subsidies gradually over several years, thus spreading the initial fiscal 'pain' to the taxpayer. But once a new policy regime is in place, it can be difficult to reverse – this is known as 'path dependence'. The reason for this path dependence is simple: politically, it is easier to increase than reduce public subsidies. This asymmetry needs to be borne in mind, especially if the scope and scale of the new subsidies are large and enjoyed by a large proportion of the electorate. Having said this, a mixed financing approach may be somewhat easier to modify than a fully publicly funded approach.

## *Coverage and access to services*

A decision to allocate government funding to a public service may be related to a desire to increase access to that service for a particular group of the population (or the whole population, in the case of universal allocation of funding). Thus, as highlighted in chapter 1, early childhood education in New Zealand is now fully funded for the first 20 hours per child. Similarly, a move to part-fund a service and require a user contribution may indicate a desire to restrict public access to a service and move that service into the sphere of private responsibility, as happened with eye tests in England. This might be based, for example, on a view that the market works perfectly well in ensuring the delivery of a particular service and a view that some services are the responsibility of individuals rather than the state.

In other cases, mixed finance may be applied in a way that enables access to services to be shaped in very specific ways, but without the state assuming full responsibility for their delivery. With legal aid in New Zealand, Australia, and England, access is clearly specified through the application of criteria to access legal aid in a general sense (through a means test) and be able to use legal aid-funded services for specific types of legal service (through a system that identifies whether particular legal services attract legal aid).

This points to the importance of evaluating a proposed approach to mixed funding in relation to its potential impact on access to, and take up of, services, as judged against government objectives for that service. For example, in exploring the potential next steps for the funding of general practice services in New Zealand, it is important to explore how recent reforms have affected people's ability to use general practice. This might suggest options for the next phase of mixed funding of general practice such as an increase in the subsidy paid to GPs (on either a universal or targeted basis); a continuation of the current approach, but with a more complete contract with doctors about what is required in return for the subsidy (for example, new or different services); and the offer to providers of the possibility of a contract to supply general practice services for certain population groups, but with no co-payment. In any evaluation of the potential impact of a mixed finance approach on access to a service, research evidence is needed about the relationship between types of finance and access to such services, together with the modelling of potential scenarios if a particular approach were to be adopted (for example, the introduction or removal of a user charge).

### Degree of choice and competition

That providers are in the private sector suggests they are likely to be operating in more and less competitive markets, seeking to attract business from consumers as fee-payers (albeit that the fee may be subsidised by state contributions), as well as from (full or part) state-funded users. Thus, the issues of competition and choice are likely to be a concern of the different stakeholders in the particular service. In deciding to use a mixed finance approach, the state is likely to want to consider how far this approach might extend or restrict competition in the market of providers, and what this might mean for the choices available to individual service users and the efficiency of the market (for example, whether prices will be artificially raised by government intervention). Considerations of choice and competition are likely to raise the issue of the appropriate regulation of the market given that users may not always have adequate information to judge the quality or price of services offered.

The approach used in New Zealand, Australia, and England for the mixed financing of long-term care for older people is an example of how the application of a government subsidy is intended to enable users to continue to exercise their choice of provider, because the subsidy, in theory, is available (on a means-tested basis) to be used in a wide variety of care facilities contracted to the state for the purpose of providing care. This example, however, does point to the need for careful evaluation of *how* such a subsidy is applied, because there is evidence that the capping of a subsidy by the government can lead to some providers exiting the market if they become financially non-viable.

## Sustaining or developing a viable market

The use of a mixed funding approach may be part of a government's attempt to develop a viable market for a public service. For example, the provision of government funding to subsidise or fully fund residential and nursing care for older people has been regarded in New Zealand, Australia, and England as being critical to ensuring adequate service provision, along with sufficient choice, given the rising demand for such care.

In 2007, district health boards attempted to tag funding for aged care providers to minimum salaries that should be paid to care home staff, with the intention of ensuring the provider market remained viable from a workforce perspective and to try to ensure an adequate standard of provision on behalf of potentially vulnerable service users. However, while providers agreed to pass on all the funding targeted for wages and be audited to ensure compliance, they rejected the district health boards' directive for a minimum sector-wide pay rate (saying they would be funded 70–80 cents but required to pass on a dollar) and new collective agreement clauses (HealthCare Providers New Zealand and Association of Residential Care Homes, 2007). When agreement could not be reached, HealthCare Providers New Zealand and the Association of Residential Care Homes took the district health boards to court and won a judicial review.[9] The review ruled that it was unlawful for the district health boards to insert clauses requiring a wage increase for providers' lower paid workers or collective agreements for those workers.

In some mixed financed services where user fees are capped, such as legal aid, it has been argued that mixed financing can threaten a viable market. Lawyers sometimes argue that the rates of subsidy the

---

9    *HealthCare Providers New Zealand Inc and New Zealand Association of Residential Care Homes Inc v Northland, Waitemata, Auckland, Counties Manukau, Waikato, Lakes, Bay of Plenty, Tairawhiti, Taranaki, Hawke's Bay, Wanganui, Midcentral, Hutt Valley, Capital & Coast, Wairarapa, Nelson Marlborough, West Coast, Canterbury, South Canterbury, Otago, and Southland District Health Boards* 7 December 2007, McGechan J, High Court Wellington CIV-2007-485-1814.

government offers make legal aid work uneconomical for lawyers to carry out unless users can be charged higher fees. While this could be seen as a threat by professionals keen to enhance their incomes, the example of dentistry in England is instructive. In this instance, many dentists stopped doing NHS work when unhappy with the level of public subsidy for adult dental care, moving their practices on to a private and fully fee-paying basis. Arguably, this has harmed access to NHS dental services in certain parts of the country.

Against this, the development of a viable market for a new public service (or one previously available only as a private good) can be initiated by a public subsidy. Examples might include the government part-funding the provision of recycling services in a community, offering vouchers for people to access low-cost swimming and exercise classes, or providing grants for the insulation of houses to reduce energy use and improve health. Although these examples are partly concerned with increasing access to, or the use of, a service, they also support the development of a robust provision of services where the market has not so far responded.

### Ability to shape services

A key consideration for the state when allocating partial funding to a public service is the extent to which it wishes to exert influence on the shape of the service and how it is delivered to users. As indicated above, the allocation of funding for 20 hours of free early childhood education in New Zealand was done in a way that clearly underlined the government's belief in the importance of teacher-led provision. In other cases, where there is a longer history of complex negotiations and relationships between providers and government (for example, with doctors and lawyers), it can prove more complicated for the state to seek to shape the nature of service provision through part-financing.

For example, the Primary Health Care Strategy in New Zealand aims to develop primary health care that is lower cost and is delivered by extensive multidisciplinary teams. Over \$2.2 billion of additional resource was allocated to primary health care over 2002–2008 to realise these aims. However, evaluations of the implementation of the Primary

Health Care Strategy suggest that, although the cost of access to general practice has been reduced and the utilisation of services has increased, the model of service provision has changed relatively little (for example, Cumming and Gribben, 2007; Cumming et al, 2008; Cumming et al, 2005; Gauld, 2008; Smith, 2008; Cumming and Mays, 2009). The reasons for this are complex and include the method by which new funding has been allocated to practices, with the use of capitation funding through an incomplete contract (Croxson et al, 2009), meaning that primary health organisations (acting as agents for the government) have had little leverage over how practices manage income and shape services.

### *Assurance of quality of services*

It is clearly important for the state to be reassured that any approach to the mixed financing of public services will promote, support, and ensure the delivery of high quality public services. In particular, the state is likely to be concerned about how service quality will be monitored, who will have access to monitoring data, and how this data will be used to improve services in line with government and professional service standards.

The state might seek to exert influence on service quality through its allocation of partial funding to private providers by, for example, specifying the staffing requirements associated with early childhood education funding in New Zealand, developing a performance management programme for primary health care in New Zealand that is applied to primary health organisations and reflects the performance of general practices, requiring legal practices in England that provide legal aid to take part in a national programme of practice accreditation, and applying an extensive service accreditation process for providers of publicly subsidised aged care services in Australia.

Such examples demonstrate how governments use mixed financing as a lever to influence not only the shape, but also the quality, of services provided to their citizens. The specific approach used for each service and country will, of necessity, vary, for it will need to achieve 'organisational fit' with the wider system of quality assessment and assurance that applies in the individual case.

## Control of entry to the market

A further consideration for the state in relation to providing funding to private providers to deliver public services (and closely related to the assurance of quality criterion), is the extent to which entry to the service market might be controlled. For example, the state may wish explicitly to restrict entry to the market through its approach to finance, applying its funding only to providers who meet certain criteria or submit to certain forms of inspection or regulation (for example, legal aid in England and early childhood education in New Zealand). On the other hand, the state may want to use mixed finance to open up entry to the market, as with the approach to funding older people's care in England. This approach was initiated in the early 1990s as an attempt to develop a market of care with more providers and hence more choices for users and to replace the previous system of largely local government provided and funded care.

## Behavioural effects of user charges

Arguments for and against user charges are typically made with significant conviction, with concerns about access for low-income people being pitched against assertions of the need to control and encourage appropriate demand, ensure consumer choice, and avoid middle-class capture. That markedly different conclusions can be reached for the same public service in different national and cultural contexts is evinced by the significant co-payments for general practice in New Zealand, the top-up co-payments in Australia, and a fully state-financed service in England.

A critical concern for the state in relation to mixed finance is to explore the rationale for any user charge, relating this rationale to its wider policy objectives, and intelligence about likely provider and user behaviour. Concerns are likely to include access to services in relation to people's ability to pay (and the need for a subsidy for some population groups), the fairness or otherwise of the financing system (for example, whether it is progressive and promotes horizontal equity), how a user charge might be regulated, and the impact of any competition law.

An example of how changing mixed finance can be particularly fraught when user charges are present is that of recently proposed changes to legal aid funding in England and New Zealand. Lawyers in these countries regarded government attempts to cap fees or to block contracting for work as a significant limitation on their professional freedom to determine how cases should be handled and a threat to the financial viability of their practices.

User charges are a complex and contested issue, especially where influential professional groups such as doctors or lawyers are the main providers of the public service under discussion. It is of note that in the other two policy areas explored in this book, early childhood education and long-term care of older people, the presence and level of user charges and the government's legitimate objective to influence charges and attach conditions to public finance appear to have been less contested. The reasons for this difference are complex. However, the reasons would seem to include the different history and make-up of the workforce (for example, law and medicine are ancient and powerful professions compared with early years education and long-term care that are provided by a mix of corporate, public, and non-governmental organisation providers using a mix of professional and support staff). Another reason may be the particularly vulnerable nature of the users of early childhood education and long-term care (where government regulation and accreditation are likely to be seen as protecting the weak).

### Cost shifting

The state needs to consider the possibility that any change to the funding of private providers might result in cost-shifting. For example, providing a subsidy for 20 hours' free early childhood education in New Zealand would seem to signal the potential for providers to increase the rates charged for hours above the subsidised hours, so they can cover any perceived gap between government funding and actual costs or to ensure income or profits. Likewise, in providing subsidies for the long-term care of older people, the New Zealand government has been keen to try to prevent providers from limiting this subsidy to a 'basic minimum' of care and charging users for 'extras' such as a single room, which might be regarded as important elements of service quality rather than something in excess of a basic package of care.

The complexity of the mixed financing of private providers of public services is likely to entail a mix of incentives that will likely see private providers attempt to shift costs. The state needs to ensure that any such behaviour is not detrimental to its overall objectives for that public service and preserves value for money in the allocation of public resources.

### Efficiency

The state needs to consider how the market for services might respond to the introduction or extension of public subsidies for public services and how such subsidies might influence productive and dynamic efficiency. A further consideration is the extent to which subsidies and user charges will influence allocative efficiency.

Allocative efficiency is achieved when the mix of services provided results in the best outcomes for the resources used. This means providing access to the most effective services and getting the balance right between different types of service. In health care, careful consideration is needed of the impact of user charges for one service on the likely demand for complementary services. For example, user charges for primary health care services may deter people from using those services while encouraging people to use free, but potentially more expensive, hospital accident and emergency services. It also means carefully considering how to encourage the use of effective services, as opposed to those services that do little good. In practice this is difficult to achieve without specifying which services can or cannot be provided through public subsidies. Such specification leads to complex regulatory or contractual arrangements (for example, the Australian Medicare Benefits Book), which may in turn reduce flexibility of care providers to best meet needs or encourage extensive cost-shifting.

## Equity

The state also needs to consider how equity (or fairness across population groups) might be affected by the different subsidy and user charge arrangements on offer.

Equity of access is generally a key goal, for example, in health services, for different population groups. Equity of access encompasses the goals of vertical equity (those with greater need having better access) and horizontal equity (those with the same needs having the same access).

Equity in the financing of services may also be a key goal for governments. This might mean the government wants to see those who can pay more contributing more to the financing of key services or it might want those who use more services to pay fully or partially for the additional services they use.

Thus, government subsidies may differ across different population groups. In New Zealand in the 1990s, for example, primary health care service subsidies differed depending on users' income while rest home subsidies are the subject of both income and asset tests, such that the government's funding is targeted towards those with lower incomes and fewer assets, as well as to those with higher needs (through a health needs assessment).

Equity of access may also be affected by supply-side considerations, so the state may need to take these into account when determining subsidy policies. For example, there may be shortages of services in particular parts of the country but not in others, and a differentiated subsidy might be an appropriate means of discouraging demand or encouraging supply in those areas where there are service shortages.

## Accountability for the use of public funds

Within a parliamentary democracy, accountability for the use of public funds is important. When designing a mixed financing regime, therefore, policy makers need to carefully consider how providers that receive public subsidies are to be held to account and whether the proposed accountability framework is consistent with the expectations of the wider political community and the norms applicable to the allocation of public funds. A potential concern in this regard is that the state might feel obliged, for reasons of parliamentary accountability and the minimisation of political risk, to develop highly specific and detailed contracts with providers. However, such contracts may result in high compliance costs for providers and limit the scope for service innovation and flexibility.

## Provider perspective

Providers consider many issues when assessing a mixed funding approach. These issues, considered briefly below, include, in no order of importance:

- acceptability
- capacity promotion
- economic viability and adequacy of resources
- professional standards and quality
- relationship with the client
- contractual relationship.

### Acceptability

For providers, a fundamental issue in the assessment of any mixed financing approach is its acceptability. Any new approach needs to be tested against professional views to determine how providers might respond to any changes and how far they might support (or inhibit) implementation.

Factors affecting acceptability to providers include the level and nature of the support to be provided for implementing a new funding approach; the perceived impact of the change on providers' day-to-day working life; the potential effect on provider income; the extent to which providers have been involved in designing the new approach; and the impact of the approach on professional concerns such as training arrangements.

Critical to this issue will be how policy makers involve leaders and representatives of provider organisations in discussions about whether, and if so, how, to introduce any financing changes. However, it should be noted that providers' initial resistance to change may not be evidence that the financing changes will not work in practice, for example, leaders of general practice in New Zealand advised their members to ignore a new scheme (Very Low Cost Access) that would entail GPs agreeing to cap the fees they charge patients in return for receiving a higher level of government subsidy. However, in the first 10 months of the scheme, 23% practices joined the scheme (Minister of Health, 2007). In July 2009, 30% of practices were in the scheme (Jo Williams, Ministry of Health, personal communication, 14 September 2009). It is important policy makers can make a judgement, working constructively with provider representatives, about how far natural human resistance to change will form part of the response to any proposed new approach and how providers will adapt to new arrangements.

### *Capacity promotion*

A key concern for providers is the extent to which a new mixed financing approach will affect workforce capacity. In all four policy areas explored in this research, New Zealand faces pressures in relation to ensuring workforce capacity to meet future service demands. Hence, providers will scrutinise any potential changes to ensure they will enhance the likelihood of people entering and staying in a particular profession.

Workforce capacity may require more sophisticated plans beyond immediate funding changes. For example, the implementation of the 20 hours of free early childhood education in New Zealand increased demand for qualified pre-school teachers, which has necessitated increases in the number of training places so future demand can be met.

Concerns about capacity also need to take account of emerging societal trends. For example, young lawyers and doctors may not want to work in the same business and ownership model as their predecessors. Therefore, what might seem unacceptable to current leaders of a profession (for example, a move away from fee-for-service private practice towards the use of block or capitated contracts or even salaried employment) might prove attractive for a newer generation less willing to own their own business, premises, or other facilities.

### Economic viability and adequacy of resources

An important test for providers (and for the state and users) is whether any new approach to mixed financing is viable. Clearly, this test forms part of the assessment of acceptability. Other considerations as part of a test of viability include any effect on transaction costs (for example, the cost of administering new arrangements in provider organisations), the implications for the long-term viability of providers (for example, making income flows more or less secure and adequate), and how far the approach will encourage new providers into the market.

Specific metrics are likely to be needed to allow robust financial comparisons between existing and proposed arrangements, including measures of transaction costs; and the likely income flows to, and costs incurred by, providers. The potential impacts on user charges and service utilisation as well as market entry exit and effort also need to be modelled.

As an example, a recent report from the English Office for Standards in Education (the national education inspectorate) found that nurseries in poorer areas were finding it more difficult to make ends meet and thus to deliver good quality care than were nurseries in wealthier areas, because poorer parents were less likely to supplement the 12.5 hours' free nursery care for their children by paying extra for a full-time place. The reverse was happening in better-off areas (Curtis, 2008).

### Professional standards and quality

Providers assess any proposed new approach to mixed finance through several lenses, including that of professional standards and quality. They are keen to ensure such standards can be upheld, or even enhanced, within new arrangements.

The area of professional standards and quality is complex and requires careful consideration of how such standards and quality are measured; without clear metrics, there is a risk of 'professional standards' being used as a reason to resist change, without clear evidence as to what these standards are. The systematic measurement of users' experiences of services is one way to mitigate such a situation, as is regular surveying of staff and trainees. The potential impact on the ability of providers to carry out training is a further area of concern, forming part of their assessment of a new financing approach.

Government funders may explicitly use professional standards as part of the process of accreditation associated with the allocation of public funding. Funders may consider such standards necessary for assuring quality in return for spending public money through private providers. For example, the legal aid system in England requires providers to undergo the Law Society's accreditation process in order to be approved as providers of publicly funded legal services. In New Zealand, the CORNERSTONE accreditation programme assesses general practices against a standard for general practice, but there is no link between meeting these standards and being able to provide publicly funded services (see RNCGP, no date)).

### *Client relationships*

For providers of services, preserving and enhancing their relationship with clients is likely to form part of their assessment of the potential impact of a change in funding approach. They may have a particular view of the role (or absence) of a co-payment in the provider–client relationship, considering this to represent something beyond a simple financial transaction. For example, New Zealand general practice leaders refer to the patient co-payment as a symbol or assurance of the integrity of the patient–professional relationship that embodies the autonomy of professionals to set their own fees, thereby preserving professional standards of care (Croxson et al, 2009). Lawyers, likewise, are accustomed to setting and charging fees. They may resent the state's move towards block contracting for their services, considering such a move might harm their relationship with clients.

On the other hand, a move to a universal subsidy such as the provision of free early childhood education in New Zealand might be viewed as removing difficult issues about fee payments, parental debts, and so forth from teachers' relationships with children and their parents.

### Contractual relationship

For providers, an issue that forms part of the acceptability criterion that was discussed earlier, but which is worthy of specific consideration, is the nature of any contract the government funder seeks to negotiate when allocating partial financing to the service. Issues of interest to the provider include the eligibility criteria in relation to becoming a provider in a mixed financing arrangement (for example, approval to be a legal aid provider in England or an early childhood education provider in the New Zealand 20 Hours Free scheme), the requirements for providing information to the government about service activity and performance, the extent of any surveying of users' experiences by funders, and the activity expected in return for entering into a contractual arrangement.

The examples of New Zealand early childhood education and long-term care and English general practice demonstrate how contracts for the public financing of private providers can be extensive in their requirements for reporting and delivery against specified indicators. Against this, approaches such as the allocation of the childcare subsidy in England require relatively little reporting by providers and have less extensive contracts underpinning the allocation of funding. More 'middle-way' approaches might include New Zealand general practice with the primary health organisation performance management programme requiring reporting to the government on aspects of primary care performance, and the Australian Medicare system where the government seeks to influence GP behaviour through the structuring of the reimbursement schedule for general practice rather than through detailed contractual reporting and monitoring.

As was seen in the typology of approaches to mixed financing explored in the previous chapter, the nature of implicit contracts varies, and this is reflected in the examples just given. When there is a clear policy intention to use the financing approach to shape service provision (as with early childhood education in New Zealand and general practice in England), the use of a detailed contract is much more likely than when the policy intention is focused on increasing access for users in general (as in New Zealand general practice and English childcare subsidies).

## User perspective

Users consider many issues when assessing a mixed funding approach. These issues, considered briefly below, include, in no order of importance:

- acceptability
- choice of provider
- equity
- quality of service
- method of payment for services
- user involvement and control.

### Acceptability

In making decisions about allocating public finance to private providers of public services, the concerns of providers rather than the concerns of actual or potential service users frequently dominate the discussion about the merits or otherwise of proposed changes. Although providers clearly have an important insight into the views of users, in the area of negotiation about financing it is important to gain independent insight into the perspective of users.

Concerns for users of public services that have mixed financing include the presence and level of any co-payment; the extent and method of any means-testing; the impact of changes to funding on how services are provided (for example, where services are based, the model of provision, and who delivers the service); and whether, and if so, how, access to services will be affected by changing the mix of public and private finance.

### Choice of provider

For users, the extent to which they can choose their provider is likely to be a concern, especially if they have traditionally had extensive choice and this will be, to some extent, circumscribed by changes to financing.

With general practice in New Zealand, although people are free to choose their practice and attend more than one practice, they are now required to be registered with a single 'home' practice, a requirement that has been sought in return for lower patient co-payments for registered patients.

With legal aid in England, choice has arguably been constrained by the requirement for providers to be accredited for legal aid funding, leading practices to opt in or out of legal aid and to specialise in certain areas where they can meet accreditation standards (and hence not provide legal services in specialist areas where they cannot be accredited). However, a trade-off clearly exists between professional standards and quality and user choice. This is an example of how the criteria in this evaluation framework sometimes have to be balanced against one another.

Although choice might be considered an inherently 'good' thing, there is evidence that people tend to be conservative in their use of public services, so that even where they have a choice, as with general practice in New Zealand and Australia, over 50% of people remain with the same provider over a long period (Schoen et al, 2004). Likewise, people may accept a restriction in choice in return for an assurance of publicly funded access to a service or a certain standard of service.

### Equity

Users are likely to have some concern for equity of access to services, especially as the extent of any public financing increases and people start to perceive the service as a 'public service' to which they are entitled in some way. For example, with the introduction of the subsidy for early childhood education in New Zealand, parent groups might initially have been grateful for any public finance, but over time, they may come to question why the state is not ensuring sufficient provision, so all parents can access such services for their children. Likewise, it will be interesting to see whether New Zealanders start to demand that everyone (or more people) can have access to the Very Low Cost Access general practice services made available in over a quarter of cases. As the government becomes a more significant funder of primary care, people may start to be concerned about who does, or does not, receive fully funded services.

This issue illustrates the importance of the state (policy makers) obtaining users' views when exploring ideas about how to use mixed financing of public services. The state is ultimately the agent of taxpayers, so the views of the population about how their public services are to be funded are a critical element when planning future funding and its application.

As with the state, users and taxpayers may also be interested in the equity of financing, expecting those who have higher incomes or more wealth to contribute more or those who use more services to pay more (in part or in full) to use such services.

### Quality of service

Service users want to know how service quality will be measured and reported and how users will be able to access such information and compare it across providers on locally and nationally. Users are also likely to want to know how they can play a part in shaping such assessment processes, possibly in partnership with government funders and representatives of provider organisations.

### Method of payment for services

Given the nature of mixed financing, users have a fundamental interest in the extent to which they are expected to make a co-payment for a service, and if so, the level of the co-payment and how it is to be made. The behavioural effects of user charges explored above form part of users' assessment of financing approaches. Any expectation of an increased user contribution is likely to come under intense public scrutiny and challenge, requiring a coherent and strong policy response. Again, the larger the proportion of public finance compared with private finance, the more users will expect the state to protect them from 'excessive' user charges.

However, in some of the services explored in this project, in particular, long-term care, legal aid, and early childhood education, service users are vulnerable and often lack advocates (albeit that parents advocate for children). By contrast, the whole population uses general practice services, which may be subject to a different degree of public engagement and concern.

### User involvement and control

Users want to be assured about the mechanisms in place to enable them to influence the implementation and review of any change to the financing of services. This points to the importance of evaluating the implementation and impact of changes on the financing of public services, examining the relationship between the approach to funding and users' experiences and service outcomes.

Many confounding factors make it difficult to carry out such an evaluation. For example, it has been asserted that changes to general practice financing in New Zealand have contributed to a reduction in the number of people reporting in the New Zealand Health Survey that cost is a barrier to their access to general practice (Ministry of Health, 2008c). However, other surveys still show high rates of unmet need (Schoen et al, 2007; Jatrana and Crampton, 2009) and primary care providers continue to report that New Zealanders defer or avoid general practice attendance for reasons of cost (Raymont and Cumming, 2009). This suggests more in-depth research among the poorest and most vulnerable members of society is needed to verify such assertions.

## Assessment framework

The criteria explored above (in relation to the state, providers, and users) are summarised in Table 5.7, and a set of tests is proposed that policy makers, providers, and user representatives could use when faced with a potential change to the mixed financing of a public service. This assessment framework is not intended to be exhaustive, but to help highlight the likely issues that will confront those making a decision about an appropriate mix of public and private financing for a particular public service.

**Table 5.7:** Framework for assessing mixed financing approaches in public services

| Criteria for assessment | Tests that might be applied |
|---|---|
| **State perspective** | |
| Fiscal costs | How much will the proposed mixed financing regime cost? |
| | How might the costs of a mixed financing regime differ from those of a fully funded approach? |
| | What longer-term fiscal risks might be associated with the proposed regime? |
| Coverage and access to services | Will the funding approach affect access to services, and if so, how? |
| Degree of choice and competition | Will the funding approach affect the extent of choice and competition within the service? |
| Sustaining or developing a viable market | Will the financing approach sustain or develop the service market in line with government objectives? |
| Ability to shape services | Will the financing approach enable the state to influence the model of service provision? |
| Assurance of quality of services | Will the financing approach enable appropriate monitoring and development of service quality? |
| Control of entry to the market | Will the funding approach affect control of entry to the service market, and if so, how? |
| Behavioural effects of user charges | How will the market be regulated? |
| | What is the rationale for any user charge? |
| | How will any user charge be regulated? |
| | Will price controls be used? |
| | What is the impact of competition law? |
| Cost-shifting | Is there potential for cost-shifting as a result of this mixed funding approach? |
| Efficiency | Will the funding approach encourage the right mix of services to be delivered? |

| Criteria for assessment | Tests that might be applied |
|---|---|
| Equity | Will the funding approach enable equity of access? Will the funding approach meet equity of financing goals (that is, will those who can afford to pay more or who are using more services pay more)? |
| Accountability | What accountability mechanisms are required under the funding approach, and how might these mechanisms affect compliance costs and the capacity of providers to innovate? |
| **Provider perspective** | |
| Acceptability | Is the funding approach likely to prove acceptable to providers? What are the implications for providers of the process of implementing the change in funding approach? |
| Capacity promotion | Will the funding approach sustain or increase workforce capacity? Will the funding approach maximise capital resources? |
| Economic viability and adequacy of resources | Is the funding approach affordable? Will the funding approach affect transaction costs? Will the funding approach affect long-term viability of providers? Will the funding approach encourage more or fewer providers into the market? |
| Professional standards and quality | Will there be any impact on professional standards and service quality? Will there be any impact on the ability to train providers? |
| Client relationship | Will there be any impact on the provider–client relationship? |
| Contractual relationship | What is the nature of any contract with the government funder? What will be the eligibility criteria for being a provider under this funding arrangement? What mechanisms will be available for providers to influence implementation and review of the approach? |

| Criteria for assessment | Tests that might be applied |
|---|---|
| **User perspectives** | |
| Acceptability | Is the level of co-payment appropriate? How might this affect patterns of service use? |
| Choice of provider | Will the funding approach affect the choice of provider? If so, how? |
| Equity | Will the funding approach affect equity of access to service provision? |
| Quality of service provision | How will service quality be reported on and assured?<br>How will users access data on quality? |
| Method of payment for services | How will users make any co-payment?<br>Will the co-payment be universal or targeted?<br>What is the nature of any means-testing? |
| User involvement and control | What mechanisms will users have available to influence the implementation and review of the funding approach? |

## Summary

In this chapter, we explored how different approaches to the mixed financing of public services might be assessed from the perspectives of the state, providers, and users.

An assessment framework set out tests that could be applied when assessing a proposed new approach to mixed financing. The criteria vary between the three perspectives, so it is to be expected that there will be debate and even conflict about alterations in the balance or method of mixed finance for a specific service. There are no simple answers to questions about whether the services discussed in this report should be financed on a mixed basis and, if so, how.

In the next chapter, we set out an example that applies the assessment framework to a specific service. This example is then used as the basis to discuss the themes raised by, and the policy implications of, this examination of approaches to mixed financing in four public services across three countries.

# 6

## Policy Implications

### Introduction

The decision to use a mix of private and public finance for a public service that is delivered by private providers reflects not only the nature of the service but a variety of factors, including government objectives for the service and the specific history of the service. By exploring four such public services in three countries, we identified different types of mixed financing. We applied this typology of mixed financing approaches to the four services in the three countries and used that analysis to inform the development of an assessment framework that might be used when alternatives to a particular approach to mixed financing of a public service are considered.

To explore the issues likely to emerge during such an assessment and what these might mean for policy options, we applied the assessment framework to the service with which the research team is most familiar – general practice in New Zealand, Australia, and England. This example is summarised in Table 6.8.

Table 6.8 is followed by an analysis of the five themes that emerge from the example. We then consider the advantages and disadvantages of using a comparative approach to identify policy implications associated with choices about approaches to mixed financing of public services.

**Table 6.8:** Application of the mixed financing assessment framework to general practice in three countries

| | New Zealand | Australia | England |
|---|---|---|---|
| Overview of mixed financing approach | Patient pays a co-payment and government pays a sum of money to the practice each year for an enrolled patient's care. Capitation approach applied to this government funding to assist with addressing health inequalities and to seek to develop more team-working and improve care of people with chronic disease. | State provides most funding for general practice visits. Providers can levy co-payments as a way of enabling choice and access to additional services. | Universal and full funding of general practice services (ie, not a mixed financing approach). |

**Criterion for assessment**

**State perspective**

| | New Zealand | Australia | England |
|---|---|---|---|
| Coverage and access to services | Funding provided to reduce the cost to users of first contact care. However, user charge still applies and may limit access. Available funding may support services where they might otherwise not exist. | Funding provided through Medicare to ensure whole population has access to general medical services. Training and funding incentives for general practitioners (GPs) to work in rural areas. | General medical services fully funded as part of a commitment to a national health service free at the point of delivery. |
| Degree of choice and competition | More choice in urban areas than in provincial areas. Some areas have closed lists. Non-governmental organisations offer alternative services for specific populations such as Māori and Pacific people. | More choice in urban areas than in rural and remote areas. Government-run and non-governmental organisations provide services for specific populations such as Aboriginal people. | Choice of general practice available in theory but not always in practice due to closed lists and enrolment 'rules'. More choice in urban areas. Alternative providers being developed in competition with practices and, for example, walk-in centres that do not require patient registration. |

| | New Zealand | Australia | England |
|---|---|---|---|
| Sustaining or developing a viable market | Additional government funding under the Primary Health Care Strategy intended to develop primary health care in line with the strategy's aims. | Additional support and incentives for rural practices. | Additional funding through general medical services contract intended to enable more 'out of hospital care' and to encourage practices to locate in less attractive areas. |
| Ability to shape services | Most public funding allocated through incomplete contract between state and practices, so restricted ability to shape services, despite capitation being used to determine level of funding. | Commonwealth government determines list of services eligible for subsidy (Medicare Benefits Schedule) and payment levels. | Extensive contract between primary care trusts and practices specifies services to be delivered, together with quality and outcome indicators. |
| Assurance of quality of services | A performance management programme is in place for primary health organisations that provide public funding to practices. The state has incomplete leverage over practice quality and relies on voluntary professional accreditation. | Practice Incentives Program provides financial incentives for practices to provide quality care. | Quality and outcomes framework of the general medical services contract entails extensive monitoring of quality within a pay-for-performance approach. Data publicly available on a practice-by-practice basis. |
| Control of entry to the market | Postgraduate GP training is not essential for GP practice, but is the norm. GPs can set up in practice according to their assessment of the local market. Capitation funding may constrain this, given a practice can access funds only if it has patients. | Postgraduate training in general practice mandatory for a GP to be granted a Medicare provider number. | Postgraduate training in general practice mandatory for a GP to receive public funding. |

|  | New Zealand | Australia | England |
|---|---|---|---|
| Behavioural effects of user charges | Fee schedules must be public. District health boards can call for a review of fee increases where increases are deemed excessive. Some practices serving high-needs populations are in a scheme where they agree to a fee cap in return for additional capitation funding.<br><br>User fee based on rationale of cost-sharing between individual and state and of enabling a consumer relationship between GP and patient. | National schedule for the reimbursement of cost of first contact care within the Medicare scheme. | Contracts for general medical services are tendered by the primary care trust, so a practice can only set up where deemed necessary by the state funder.<br><br>No user charges are levied – universal public funding of general practice services (with the exception of prescription charges). |
| Cost shifting | Potential for GPs to close books when they have sufficient enrolees to secure capitation income and to 'cream skim' healthier patients. | No incentive to cost shift since GPs are paid per episode of care. | Some concern whether practices 'cream skim' to secure maximum Quality and Outcomes Framework points, but no evidence found of this. |
| Efficiency | General practice user charges may encourage service users to inappropriately use hospital-based accident and emergency services, which are free to the service user, resulting in an inefficient allocation of resources. | Medical treatment largely subsidised and its use largely unlimited. | No incentive to use hospital services over GP services because both are free at point of use. |

| | New Zealand | Australia | England |
|---|---|---|---|
| Equity | Charges patients pay are determined by service providers, so they can decide to keep charges low for patients they know may not be able to afford care, which may promote equity of access.<br><br>With patient user charges, those who use more services pay more, promoting equity in financing. | A Medicare Safety Net operates for individuals and families who reach a threshold for out-of-pocket costs. Those eligible are then entitled to higher Medicare benefits. | |

**Provider perspective**

| | New Zealand | Australia | England |
|---|---|---|---|
| Acceptability | Practices resistant to perceived control of fees, yet content to accept additional funding from state to reduce fees charged to users. Complaints about bureaucracy of the system, including use of multiple parallel funding streams. | Initial opposition by medical profession to the introduction of universal compulsory health insurance in the 1970s. | Profession voted by a large majority to accept new General Medical Services contract in 2003. GPs have experienced significant increases in income as a result of new contract. |
| Capacity promotion | Additional funding has enabled increase in number of practice nurses and extra services provided through practices such as health promotion and chronic diseases management. | Practice Incentives Program provides additional payments for accredited practices. Includes a practice nurse incentive (including other allied health workers and Aboriginal health workers) and rural loading payment. | Additional funding and contract appear to have addressed workforce issues. Question as to whether this will persist over the longer term. |
| Economic viability and adequacy of resources | Additional public funding has enabled fee reductions and addressed some general practice concerns about viability, but questions remain about how to sustain approach in longer term. | Under a fee-for-service system, viability depends on how adequately the fee per service matches the cost of providing that service. | Appears to have addressed many concerns about viability of general practice. Little current debate about viability. |

|  | New Zealand | Australia | England |
|---|---|---|---|
| Professional standards and quality | Primary health organisation performance management programme intended to affect service quality in line with overall government health targets. Medical profession argues co-payment acts as incentive for professionals to treat patients as consumers. | Professional accreditation and standards. Divisions of general practice performance programme. | Evidence from evaluation of the General Medical Services contract and Quality and Outcomes Framework is that quality standards have been improved and that this is more pronounced in high needs localities. Assessment of primary care trusts and primary care services by the Care Quality Commission (health and social care regulator). |
| Client relationship | Patient still pays a fee to GP, although this is not now such a significant element of overall GP income. Capitation basis of state funding may encourage more proactive and preventive care. | GPs may charge a patient co-payment in addition to claiming the Medicare Benefits Schedule fee. As a non-capitated system, there is less funding incentive for preventive care. | Patients arguably more likely to receive proactive and preventive care as required under the General Medical Services contract, in comparison with arrangements before 2004. |
| Contractual relationship | Incomplete contract between district health boards and primary health organisations in respect of public funding allocated for first contact care. Includes requirement to ensure increased subsidy payments result in contracted providers charging enrolled patients low or reduced fees that are 'fair to the providers and reasonable to the patients'. | National agreement between federal government and practices for Medicare funding. | Complete contract between primary care trust and individual practice. |

| | New Zealand | Australia | England |
|---|---|---|---|
| **User perspective** | | | |
| Acceptability | Reduced fees for most people, and evidence of increased service utilisation and of cost being less of a barrier in respect of access to services. | State provides funding for what it deems to be core primary health care services, but expects the user to pay for additional services. | Strong public support for 'free' GP services. |
| Choice of provider | Patient can choose their practice and to consult another practice. However, closed GP lists restrict such choice in some areas. Capitation funding may encourage closure of lists, when adequate funding has been secured for practice population. This may also dissuade new practices from opening, because they need assured flow of capitation funding (ie, a patient list) to be viable. | Patients can choose their GP and are not required to register. Choice may be limited in rural areas. | To promote greater choice, patients recently given right to change practice without having to give a reason. |
| Equity | Evidence of high-needs groups consulting general practice more and fewer people reporting cost as a barrier to access. However, fee reductions have been greater for the well-off, given the universal approach to application of new funding. | Poorer health and less access to services by indigenous Australians and people living in rural areas. Training and funding incentives for GPs to work in rural areas. Commonwealth funding for additional community-based services for indigenous Australians. | Universal funding intended to address equity concerns, but evidence of more GP availability in affluent areas. |

| | New Zealand | Australia | England |
|---|---|---|---|
| Quality of service provision | *See state and provider sections on quality* | *See state and provider sections on quality* | *See state and provider sections on quality* |
| Method of payment for services | User pays a fee to provider. Fee is determined by provider as a commercial decision. Provider receives capitation funding from the state with the intention of that funding enabling user fees to be kept to a lower level than would otherwise be the case. | Doctors may bulk-bill Medicare for Medicare Benefits Schedule fees, or they may charge the patient, who then claims back the cost from Medicare. Doctors may also charge additional patient fees. | GPs receive funding from the government through a contract held with the local primary care trust. No charges are made by practices to users. |
| User involvement and control | Community representation on board of primary health organisation that funds primary care services locally. | Independent non-governmental organisation, the Consumers Health Forum of Australia, provides a consumer voice for health policy and programme development. | Community representation on the board of primary care trust that funds primary care locally. Patient experience survey results increasingly being used as part of the GMS contract, connected to payments to practices for performance. |

## Assessing approaches to mixed financing of general practice

The application (in Table 6.8) of the mixed financing assessment framework to general practice reveals important implications for users, providers, and the state of selecting different approaches and the value of making comparisons of across countries.

### *Role of financing in assuring access and quality*

Our analysis of how New Zealand, Australia, and England finance general practice services underlines the critical importance of the value the governments of these countries give to ensuring public access to such services. In each country, public funding is allocated with the intention of ensuring that as many of the population as possible have access to core general practice services. Thus, England has chosen to provide universal free access to general practice, Australia uses the Medicare system to enable universal access to a minimum level of general practice provision (with regulated co-payments for additional services), and New Zealand provides a universal subsidy but without formal fee regulation to try to ensure low-cost access to general practice.

What differs across the countries is not only how they allocate a mix of public and private finance, but also how far they have used the funding approach to bring about other government objectives such as changes to service models or assurance of certain levels of quality. In England, the move to connect high levels of and large increases in public finance with requirements on general practices to demonstrate quality and performance has been explicit. In New Zealand and Australia, the state appears reluctant to require general practices to provide information about quality and performance. Both countries have attempted to develop performance management programmes for primary care, but have done so at the level of the intermediary organisation rather than directly with practices (for example, by using the New Zealand primary health organisation and the Australian division of general practice as the body whose performance the state measures and rewards).

## *Importance of context*

This illustrates how, despite a common concern about such issues, what is acceptable to the government and the public varies. The analysis in Table 6.8 demonstrates how policy is inevitably implemented within a specific context.

In the example of general practice, the context is the profession of general practice. In particular, the business model in which the profession operates is critical. In all three countries, the way the profession of general practice negotiated its business arrangements when a public health system was established continues to have a direct impact on how the state now elects to finance primary care services. Thus, the 'deals' struck in the 1930s and 1940s continue to play a part in determining what the profession, the government, and the public consider to be acceptable levels and allocations of state finance. Most vividly, New Zealand GPs (and perhaps some of the public) appear to place a high value on the ability of GPs to charge patients a co-payment within a consumer relationship, while in England, GPs and patients alike consider the absence of any payment within the doctor–patient relationship to be a core and cherished value (Secretary of State for Health, 2008).

## *Extent and nature of contracting*

Our analysis of general practice financing underlines the importance of deciding how the state will contract with private providers when allocating public funding with the intention of achieving certain public policy objectives. For example, in England a complete and extensive pay-for-performance contract is in place between the state and general practice. It is a contract that rests on full state finance. Although not an example of mixed financing, we included English general practice in our analysis to demonstrate how a government can elect to use the allocation of new public funds as an opportunity to draw a profession into a more closely regulated contractual environment, albeit with significant incentives and income attached.

In New Zealand, despite the allocation of additional public funding with the intention of reducing patient co-payments, the contract between the state and GPs remains partial, being between district health boards and primary health organisations and not directly with practices. The contract is also highly incomplete in that it does not make explicit what the state requires in terms of service delivery in return for the allocation of government funding (beyond an implied desire for lower patient fees, as evinced in a process for reviewing local fees). Instead, the government relies on a capitation approach to allocating money to primary health organisations in the hope that it will lead to desired changes in the model of care.

In Australia, meanwhile, the federal government has chosen to use the Medicare reimbursement schedule to incentivise change within primary care, thus using the financing and contractual environment to signal desired changes in service provision. However, the use of the reimbursement schedule for this purpose appears to have limitations. It seems the federal government is increasingly contracting with practices through the intermediary of GP networks that organise and support general practice at a local level. This points to the potential for government to contract not only with general practices as single providers, but also with their overarching or intermediary bodies. In a policy environment where primary care is expected to deliver a wider range of more complex services, this example of extended primary care contracting in Australia appears to parallel current discussion in New Zealand about integrated family health centres and primary care networks.

### Significance of user charges

A critical area of difference between the three countries' approaches to financing general practice is the existence or otherwise of a user charge and the proportion of total GP income represented by any such charge. Thus, in England, the absence of a user charge and the presence of full government funding clearly lend the state a degree of influence over general practice finance and provision that is not present in New Zealand and Australia. In New Zealand and Australia, for reasons of history and context, general practice has retained greater autonomy from the state; autonomy that is made manifest in the freedom to charge patients directly.

As noted in chapter 2, if a user charge is retained, it can represent an attempt to shape demand for a service (typically to avoid 'inappropriate use') and is a demonstration by the state of its desire for users to share in the cost of a service. Our analysis of how mixed financing affects general practice also points to the role of a user charge in limiting the influence the state might have on the shape and quality of service, especially where (as in New Zealand) the user charge remains a significant element of providers' income and hence the state contribution is partial. In Australia, where the state contributes 100% of the cost of GP visits for many people, the potential to influence service delivery models is arguably greater than in New Zealand.

It is clear that a user charge represents more than a financial contribution. It is a metaphor for a user contribution to (and potentially control of) a public service (Croxson et al, 2009) and of a professional's ability to have a direct business relationship with a service user as a paying client. Where a user is not only a recipient (and an arguably passive recipient) of services, but also a consumer who pays for those services, the state is likely to have less influence over service provision and quality. However, the user, in principle, should have more power and choice, assuming the user is given plenty of relevant information and can judge the appropriateness and quality of the services on offer. It should be borne in mind that the tests of equity set out in Table 6.8 illustrate that where a co-payment is in place, people on lower incomes are likely to be disadvantaged in respect of such power and choice.

### *Nature of user involvement and control*

Within our assessment of the mixed financing of general practice in three countries, service users emerge as having relatively little involvement in, or control over, the funding arrangements and associated issues of regulation, quality control, service design, and so forth. Much of the analysis is concerned with the state–provider (in this case, general practitioner) relationship, and users appear comparatively powerless in respect of shaping how services are delivered and to what standard. Instead, a powerful profession appears to have succeeded in securing significant autonomy and self-determination while receiving public funding in return for relatively little specification or monitoring as to how that funding is used (except in England).

Within long-term care of older people and early childhood education in New Zealand, service providers have markedly less autonomy than is the case with GPs. In the former services, it appears the state has chosen to advocate for service users through the contracting process, by incorporating stringent quality and other requirements into contracts with providers. The use of mixed financing is clearly an opportunity for governments to act on behalf of service users to try to ensure quality and shape service provision. However, in the presence of powerful professions, it appears that the state's willingness or capacity to assume such an advocacy role may be compromised. This may point to the need for alternative means of user empowerment, including the use of co-payments, service vouchers, or (supported) user choice. Another approach, which the NHS is using in England, is to tie patient-reported outcomes and patients' experiences of services to part of the payment received by hospitals and general practices, respectively.

### Summary of themes emerging from application of the assessment framework

Our application of the assessment framework for mixed financing approaches has revealed five key issues that appear to be of particular note when exploring the advantages and disadvantages of approaches to mixed financing of public services delivered by private providers. The issues are the:

- role of financing in assuring access, quality, and value for money
- importance of context
- extent and nature of contracting
- significance of user charges
- nature of user involvement and control.

In the next part of this chapter, we discuss what we have learned from making international and cross-sectoral comparisons of mixed financing, before drawing overall conclusions.

## Comparing mixed financing approaches on an international and cross-sectoral basis

A careful comparative assessment of the approach to the mixed financing of a particular service offers insights into alternative ways in which a service might address the five issues listed above. For example, the New Zealand early childhood education policy of a phased move towards teacher-led provision by all centres that access state finance challenges English policy in terms of how the process of allocating state finance for early years' provision could be more closely linked to quality criteria such as workforce composition. Recent developments in English legal aid similarly provide an insight for New Zealand as to how contracting and provider accreditation could be used in a more extensive manner when allocating public money to private providers of legal services.

Comparisons within a country and across sectors are also instructive, as was evinced with the application of our proposed assessment framework to the financing arrangements of general practice across three countries. For example, some commentators and analysts of social and educational policy have expressed concern that the 20 hours' free early childhood education could encourage potential cost-shifting by providers if they perceive the finance from the state to be inadequate and increase fees for hours in addition to the state-funded 20 (Early Childhood Council, 2007a, 2007b; de Raad, 2005). This echoes a concern about what might have happened to finance allocated for first-contact general practice care in New Zealand, and how far funding has or has not been passed onto users in the form of reduced fees. In both cases, providers argue that their costs need to be more fully funded and that new public money is to address the pressures they were already facing.

A comparison of the two experiences offers insight into alternative approaches to allocating new public finance and managing this allocation alongside a system of user fees that private providers set and levy. The health system in New Zealand is using a fees review process for those practices considered to be outliers. The process is administered through district health boards. The Ministry of Education, meanwhile, is using regulation as its main policy tool to ensure that money in the early childhood education sector goes where it is intended. Regulation is being used to tie new funding to staffing requirements. The ministry is undertaking a detailed national analysis of costs and the workforce to support this approach.

Comparisons of a particular sector across all three countries offer insights into the areas of commonality that in turn affect the approach to mixed funding. Examples here include the desire by general practitioners and lawyers to retain professional autonomy, and for this autonomy to include how they determine their patient or client base, charge fees, and decide how a particular patient or client's care or case should be handled. This comparison highlights issues of professional power and influence. It is interesting to note that where the government in England has sought to use more extensive national contracting to underpin its allocation of public money for general practice and legal aid, this approach has not been deemed appropriate in New Zealand. Australia, however, appears to have taken something of a 'third way' to mixed financing arrangements for professionally dominated public services. The Australian approach sits between the approaches of England and New Zealand, with general practices subject to a negotiated national framework for public finance (albeit with freedom to charge additional co-payments) and a mix of directly provided state legal services and contracted work from private lawyers.

## Policy implications

Our comparison of approaches to mixed financing across four public services in three countries has enabled us to develop a generic typology of these financing approaches. We have also developed an assessment framework that policy makers might use to assess, from state, provider, and user perspectives, the advantages and disadvantages of different mixed public and private financing options for public services.

We offer the typology and assessment framework as tools to be applied within a particular public policy and national context and with no value judgements as to what the 'right' answer might be in terms of the balance between public and private finance.

Of particular note within our comparative study has been the potential for governments to use mixed financing to try to fulfil objectives related to access and quality. Critical to such decisions will be the specific historical and national context of the service under consideration, as evinced when applying assessment criteria such as acceptability to professionals and users, economic viability, and behavioural effects of user charges. The use of contracts is an issue that recurs throughout this study, including how complete or otherwise a state–provider contract is and how far the state uses any contract in relation to service regulation and monitoring.

In respect of user charges, our summary of research suggests that, although co-payments can enable consumers to exert some pressure on providers in relation to choice and can deter 'inappropriate' service use, they also entail a variety of potential unintended effects, such as preventing access to services by those in most need or of the least means, and make contracts and other regulatory mechanisms more complicated to implement.

Perhaps the most striking policy implication from our study is the lack of any significant user involvement in, or control of, the financing and planning of the services we examined. Our exploration of how mixed financing is used focused, not by design, almost exclusively on state–provider relationships, both in the interviews we carried out earlier in this research and in the stakeholder workshop held to discuss emerging findings. This raises an important challenge for governments and service providers alike: when discussing how best to finance a public service, how can the user experience and voice be brought to bear? Governments and professions alike will frequently refer to the benefit for users when making their cases, but this study demonstrates how, when financing options are examined, the user is likely to have the least say in what happens.

This study has demonstrated the potential for comparing public service financing within and across countries. In particular, the potential to be gained from cross-sectoral comparisons within a country has been highlighted, something that is relatively rare, since policy makers tend to remain within their particular area and may be more ready to look internationally for comparisons than to look for inspiration from other service areas in their own country. Although the connections between early childhood education, legal aid, the long-term care of older people, and general practice may not be immediately apparent, using the lens of mixed financing enables generic categories of financing to be identified, together with criteria by which such financing options might be assessed.

As set out in chapter 2, decisions about financing methods are fundamental to public policy and management and involve inevitable trade-offs between competing priorities and interests. This scoping study has been undertaken to examine the potential that might be gained from taking an international and cross-sectoral comparative approach to policy analysis of service financing.

We offer the resulting typology of approaches to mixed financing and assessment framework to stimulate discussion and in the hope that they will be used in what is a complex and fraught area. Proposals to alter how a public service delivered by private providers is financed will inevitably lead to heated debate. If the typology and assessment framework developed within this small comparative study can play some part in enabling a cooler assessment of options, then the study will have achieved its purpose.

## Suggestions for further research

This study on managing mixed financing of privately owned providers in the public interest reveals ideas for future research.

Other areas of policy where mixed financing arrangements are in place (such as tertiary education, integrated schools, and accident compensation) could be explored further to identify other reasons for, and consequences of, this financing approach.

A more detailed literature review could be undertaken to seek empirical evidence about the impact of different models on the criteria for assessment set out in this book. The identification of key gaps in knowledge as a result of the literature review may reveal other areas for further research.

The design of financing arrangements also needs to take into account the insights of social psychology and behavioural economics.

Finally, new applied research to examine the costs and outcomes of different financing approaches in New Zealand is needed to help guide policy makers when the government is funding private providers to deliver public services. Of particular interest is whether different financing arrangements result in different outcomes, including overall cost, coverage, quality, and efficiency.

# References

2025 Taskforce (2009) *Answering the $64,000 Question: Closing the income gap with Australia by 2025 – First report and recommendations 2025 Taskforce.* Wellington: New Zealand Government. www.2025taskforce.govt.nz/pdfs/2025tf-1streport-nov09.pdf.

ADLS Public Issues Committee (1989) *Legal Aid in New Zealand and its Objectives.* Auckland: Auckland District Law Society.

Aged Care Standards and Accreditation Agency Ltd (no date) *Accreditation Standards.* www.accreditation.org.au/AccreditationStandards (accessed 15 March 2010).

Ashton, T (2000) 'New Zealand: Long-term care in a decade of change.' *Health Affairs* 19(3): 72–85.

Australian Government DEEWR (Department of Education Employment and Workplace Relations) (no date, a) *Information for Families Using Child Care.* www.oececc.gov.au/child_care/fact_sheets.htm (accessed 25 September 2008).

Australian Government DEEWR (Department of Education Employment and Workplace Relations) (no date, b) *Information for Families Using Child Care.* www.deewr.gov.au/EarlyChildhood/Resources/Documents/FactSheets/Info forfamiliesfactsheet.pdf (accessed 15 March 2010).

Australian Government DHA (Department of Health and Ageing) (2007) *Improving the Quality of Residential Care: Residential care standards and accreditation.* www.health.gov.au/internet/main/publishing.nsf/Content/ageing-rescare-standard.htm (accessed 15 March 2010).

Australian Government DHA (Department of Health and Ageing) (2009a) *Community Aged Care Packages.* www.health.gov.au/internet/main/publishing.nsf/Content/ageing-publicat-brochure-ccp.htm (accessed 15 March 2010).

Australian Government DHA (Department of Health and Ageing) (2009b) *Home-Based Care: Care recipient contributions and subsidies for community care packages.* http://www.health.gov.au/internet/main/publishing.nsf/Content/ageing-commcare-comcprov-ccpindex.htm (accessed 15 March 2010).

Australian Government DHA (Department of Health and Ageing) (2009c) *Home-Based Care: Extended aged care at home packages.* www.health.gov.au/internet/main/publishing.nsf/Content/ageing-commcare-comcprov-eachdex.htm (accessed 15 March 2010).

Australian Government DHA (Department of Health and Ageing) (2010a) *About the PBS.* www.health.gov.au/internet/main/publishing.nsf/Content/health-pbs-general-aboutus.htm-copy2 (accessed 15 March 2010).

Australian Government DHA (Department of Health and Ageing) (2010b) *About the PBS: Safety net.* www.health.gov.au/internet/main/publishing.nsf/Content/health-pbs-general-safetynet.htm (accessed 15 March 2010).

Australian Government DHA (Department of Health and Ageing) (2010c) *Fees and Charges for Residential Aged Care: An overview.* Information sheet no 9. Canberra: Australian Government Department of Health and Ageing. www.health.gov.au/internet/main/publishing.nsf/Content/38A97C5DDFEB 223ACA25744000810E58/$File/Info09.pdf (accessed 15 March 2010).

Burton, M (2006) *More New Zealanders Eligible for Legal Aid.* www.beehive.govt.nz/release/more+new+zealanders+eligible+legal+aid (accessed 15 March 2010).

Bushouse, BK (2008) *Early Childhood Education Policy in Aotearoa/New Zealand: The creation of the 20 Hours Free programme.* Wellington: Fulbright New Zealand.

Bushouse, BK (2009) 'The 20 Hours (Free) programme.' *Policy Quarterly* 5(1): 58–63.

Cabinet Business Committee (2006a) *Free Early Childhood Education: Approval of funding rates* CBC (06) 366. Wellington: Cabinet Office.

Cabinet Business Committee (2006b) *Minute of Decision: Free early childhood education – Approval of funding rates* CBC Min (06) 23/8. Wellington: Cabinet Office.

Care Quality Commission (no date) *Making a Difference to People's Lives through Modern Health Care and Social Care Regulation.* www.cqc.org.uk/_db/_documents/Making_a_Difference.pdf (accessed 9 March 2010).

Caring Choices (2008) *The Future of Care Funding: Time for a change* www.kingsfund.org.uk/applications/research/index.rm?id=38&skip=0&filt er=publications&count=100&sort=date (accessed 15 March 2010).

Catherall, S (2009) 'Winners and losers.' *The Dominion Post: Your weekend magazine* 1 August, pp 6–9.

Citizens Advice Bureau (2010) *Benefits in England: Benefits and tax credits for people in work.* www.adviceguide.org.uk/index/life/benefits/benefits_and_tax_credits_for_ people_in_work.htm (accessed 15 March 2010).

Croxson, B, J Smith, and J Cumming (2009) *Patient Fees as a Metaphor for so Much More in New Zealand's Primary Health System.* Wellington: Health Services Research Centre, Victoria University of Wellington.

Cumming, J, and B Gribben (2007) *Evaluation of the Primary Health Care Strategy: Practice data analysis 2001–2005.* Wellington and Auckland: Health Services Research Centre and CBG Ltd.

Cumming, J, and N Mays (2009) 'New Zealand's Primary Health Care Strategy: Early effects of the new financing and payment system for general practice and future challenges.' *Health Economics, Policy and Law* doi:10.1017/S1744133109990260.

Cumming, J, N Mays, and B Gribben (2008) 'Reforming primary health care: Is New Zealand's primary health care strategy achieving its early goals?' *Australia and New Zealand Health Policy* 5(24), doi:10.1186/1743-8462-5-24. www.anzhealthpolicy.com/content/pdf/1743-8462-5-24.pdf.

Cumming, J, A Raymont, B Gribben, M Horsburgh, B Kent, et al (2005) *Evaluation of the Implementation and Intermediate Outcomes of the Primary Health Care Strategy.* Wellington: Health Services Research Centre, Victoria University of Wellington.

Curtis, P (2008) 'Ofsted highlights nurseries divide.' *The Guardian* 10 November. www.guardian.co.uk/education/2008/nov/10/early-years-education-nurseries (accessed 15 March 2010).

Daycare Trust (2010) *Help with Childcare Costs for Working Parents* www.daycaretrust.org.uk/data/files/Information_Services/Factsheets/help_ with_childcare_costs_for_working_parents_jan10.pdf (accessed 15 March 2010).

de Raad, J-P (2005) *Early Childhood Participation: Is '20 Free Hours' the answer?* Report prepared for the Early Childhood Council. Wellington: New Zealand Institute of Economic Research.

Department for Constitutional Affairs (2005) *A Fairer Deal for Legal Aid.* London: Department for Constitutional Affairs.

Department for Constitutional Affairs (2006) *Legal Aid: A sustainable future.* Consultation paper CP13/06. London: Department for Constitutional Affairs.

Department for Constitutional Affairs and Legal Services Commission (2006) *Legal Aid Reform: The way ahead.* London: Department for Constitutional Affairs and Legal Services Commission.

DHBNZ (District Health Boards New Zealand) (no date) *PHO Performance Programme.* www.dhbnz.org.nz/Site/SIG/pho (accessed 15 March 2010).

Donaldson, C, and K Gerard (2005) *Economics of Health Care Financing: The visible hand* (2nd ed). Basingstoke, Hampshire: Palgrave Macmillan.

Early Childhood Council (2007a) *Centres Opt in by Transferring Charges.* http://www.ecc.org.nz/mediareleases/index.php?rt=20&rid=1033 (accessed 15 June 2010).

Early Childhood Council (2007b) *Parents Paying for 'Free' ECE by Variety of Methods.* http://www.ecc.org.nz/mediareleases/index.php?rt=20&rid=1032 (accessed 15 June 2010).

Ellins, J, C Ham, and H Parker (2008) *Choice and Competition in Primary Care: Much ado about nothing?* Birmingham: Health Services Management Centre.

Fine, M (1999) *The Responsibility for Child and Aged Care: Shaping policies for the future.* Sydney: Social Policy Research Centre, University of New South Wales.

Froese, N. (2008) *Early Effects of Free Early Childhood Education.* Wellington: Ministry of Education.

Gauld, R. (2008) 'The unintended consequences of New Zealand's primary health care reforms.' *Journal of Health Politics, Policy and Law* 33(1): 93–115.

Glasby, J, and R Littlechild (2000) 'Fighting fires? Emergency hospital admission and the concept of prevention.' *Journal of Management in Medicine* 14(2): 109–118.

Glasby, J, R Littlechild, and K Pryce (2006) 'All dressed up but nowhere to go? Delayed hospital discharges and older people.' *Journal of Health Services Research and Policy* 11(1): 52–58.

Griffiths, R (1988) *Community Care: Agenda for action.* London: HMSO.

Gruber, J (2006) *The Role of Consumer Copayments for Health Care: Lessons from the RAND health insurance experiment and beyond.* California: Kaiser Family Foundation.

HealthCare Providers New Zealand and Association of Residential Care Homes (2007) *Aged Care Legal Case about Ministerial Openness and Accountability.* Media release, 18 November 2007. http://healthcareproviders.org.nz/media/documents/HCPNZandARCHStatement.pdf (accessed 15 March 2010).

Healy, J, E Sharman, and B Lokuge (2006) *Australia: Health system review.* Copenhagen: European Observatory on Health Care Systems.

Hirsch, D (2005) *Facing the Cost of Long-Term Care: Towards a sustainable funding system.* York: Joseph Rowntree Foundation. www.jrf.org.uk/sites/files/jrf/1859353894.pdf (accessed 15 March 2010).

Hirsch, D (2006) *Five Costed Reforms to Long-Term Care Funding.* York: Joseph Rowntree Foundation. www.jrf.org.uk/sites/files/jrf/long-term-care-costings.pdf (accessed 15 March 2010).

HM Government (2009) *Shaping the Future of Care Together.* London: HM Government.

Jatrana, S, and P Crampton (2009) 'Primary health care in New Zealand: Who has access?' *Health Policy* 93(1): 1–10.

Joseph Rowntree Foundation (2006) *Paying for Long-Term Care: Moving forward.* www.jrf.org.uk/sites/files/jrf/0186.pdf (accessed 15 March 2010).

Keeler, EB (1995) 'A model of demand for effective care.' *Journal of Health Economics* 14(2): 231–238.

Kwon, Y-I (2002) 'Changing curriculum for early childhood education in England.' *Early Childhood Research and Practice* 4(2). Retrieved from http://ecrp.uiuc.edu/v4n2/kwon.html.

Le Quesne, K (2006) *Education Report: Progress on free ECE funding rates.* FP 25/07/07/1. Wellington: Ministry of Education.

Legal Aid Review (2009a) *Improving the Legal Aid System: A public discussion paper.* Wellington: Ministry of Justice.

Legal Aid Review (2009b) *Transforming the Legal Aid System: Final report and recommendations*. Wellington: Ministry of Justice.

Legal Services Agency (no date, a) *Criminal Legal Aid*. www.lsa.govt.nz/legal-aid/legal-aid-guide/criminal/who-pays.php (accessed 15 March 2010).

Legal Services Agency (no date, b) *Legal Services*. www.lsa.govt.nz/about-us/legal-services/legal-services.php (accessed 15 March 2010).

Legal Services Agency (no date, c) *Welcome to the Legal Services Agency*. www.lsa.govt.nz/index.php (accessed 15 March 2010).

Legal Services Commission (2007a) *Paying for Your Legal Aid*. London: Legal Services Commission.

Legal Services Commission (2007b) *A Practical Guide to Criminal Defence Services*. London: Legal Services Commission.

Legal Services Commission (2007c) *A Step-by-Step Guide to Legal Aid: Help with paying for civil cases*. London: Legal Services Commission and Ministry of Justice.

Lexchin, J, and P Grootendorst (2004) 'Effects of prescription drug user fees on drug and health services use and on health status in vulnerable populations: a systematic review of the evidence.' *International Journal of Health Services* 34(1): 101–122.

Lynch, J (2001) 'Early Australian statutory legal aid schemes and the legal profession.' Special Issue: For the public good – pro bono and the legal profession in Australia. *Law in Context* 19: 138–147.

Medicare Australia (2009a) *How Does Medicare Work?* www.medicareaustralia.gov.au/public/register/how-works.jsp (accessed 15 March 2010).

Medicare Australia (2009b) *Medicare*. www.medicareaustralia.gov.au/about/whatwedo/medicare.jsp (accessed 15 March 2010).

Medicare Australia (2009c) *What Medicare Covers*. www.medicareaustralia.gov.au/public/claims/what-cover.jsp (accessed 15 March 2010).

Medicare Australia (2010) *Medicare Safety Net*. www.medicareaustralia.gov.au/public/services/msn/index.jsp (accessed 15 March 2010).

# References

Minister of Education (A Tolley) (2009) *Budget Boost for Education Priorities.* www.beehive.govt.nz/release/budget+boost+education+priorities (accessed 15 March 2010).

Minister of Health (A King) (2001) *The Primary Health Care Strategy.* Wellington: Ministry of Health.

Minister of Health (P Hodgson) (2005) *Budget 2005 Health Overview: Speech Notes for Budget lockup briefing on health measures in Budget 2005.* www.beehive.govt.nz/node/23144 (accessed 15 March 2010).

Minister of Health (P Hodgson) (2007) *Lower Fees to See the Doctor.* www.beehive.govt.nz/node/30439 (accessed 17 August 2009).

Ministry for Culture and Heritage (2007) *Education: Children and adolescents, 1930–60.* www.nzhistory.net.nz/culture/children-and-adolescents-1940-60/education (accessed 15 March 2010).

Ministry of Education (2002) *Pathways to the Future: Ngā Huarahi Arataki.* Wellington: Ministry of Education.

Ministry of Education (2007a) *Briefing to the Education and Science Select Committee: Free ECE.* Wellington: Ministry of Education.

Ministry of Education (2007b) *Free ECE: Information for parents.* Wellington: Ministry of Education.

Ministry of Education (2008) *Briefing to the Incoming Minister.* Wellington: Ministry of Education.

Ministry of Health (2006) *PHO Service Agreement: Fees review process referenced document.* Version 1.0. www.moh.govt.nz/moh.nsf/pagesmh/5517/$File/pho-service-agreement-fees-review-process.pdf (accessed 15 March 2010).

Ministry of Health (2007a) *Looking at Long-Term Residential Care in a Rest Home or Continuing Care Hospital: What you need to know.* www.moh.govt.nz/moh.nsf/indexmh/long-term-residential-care-mar07-online#financialassessment (accessed 15 March 2010).

Ministry of Health (2007b) *Primary Health Care Pharmaceutical Subsidy Card.* www.moh.govt.nz/moh.nsf/indexmh/phcs-funding-psc (accessed 15 March 2010).

Ministry of Health (2008a) *Health Expenditure Trends in New Zealand 1996–2006.* Wellington: Ministry of Health.

Ministry of Health (2008b) *Health of Older People in New Zealand: Questions and answers on residential care.* www.moh.govt.nz/moh.nsf/UnidPrint/MH5643?OpenDocument (accessed 15 March 2010).

Ministry of Health (2008c) *A Portrait of Health: Key results of the 2006/07 New Zealand Health Survey.* Wellington: Ministry of Health.

Ministry of Health (2009) *Very Low Cost Access Payments.* www.moh.govt.nz/moh.nsf/indexmh/phcs-projects-lowcost (accessed 15 March 2010).

Morrison, A (2008) *Impact of 20 Hours ECE on Playcentres.* Wellington: Ministry of Education.

Mossialos, E, A Dixon, J Figueras, and J Kutzin (2002) *Funding Health Care: Options for Europe.* Policy brief no 4. Copenhagen: European Observatory on Health Care Systems.

New Zealand Kindergartens (no date) *History.* www.nzkindergarten.org.nz/about/history.html (accessed 15 March 2010).

New Zealand Playcentre Federation (no date) *History.* www.playcentre.org.nz/history.php (accessed 15 March 2010).

NHS (National Health Service) (2009) *Help with Health Costs.* www.nhs.uk/NHSEngland/Healthcosts/Pages/Prescriptioncosts.aspx (accessed 15 March 2010).

Noone, MA (2001) 'The state of Australian legal aid.' *Federal Law Review* 29(1): 37–56.

Office of the Minister of Education and Office of the Acting Minister for Social Development and Employment (2004) *Early Childhood Education Funding: Additional Information.* POL (04) 71. Wellington: Cabinet Policy Committee.

Pollock, S (1975) *Legal Aid: The first 25 years.* London: Oyez Publishing.

Raymont, A, and Cumming, J (2009) *Status and Activities of General Medical Practices.* Wellington: Health Services Research Centre.

Regan, C (2007) *Legal Services Commission England and Wales: National report.* Antwerp, Belgium: International Legal Aid Group Conference.

RNCGP (Royal New Zealand College of General Practitioners) (no date) *CORNERSTONE.* www.rnzcgp.org.nz/cornerstone (accessed 15 March 2010).

# References

Robinson, P (2004) *How Do We Pay? Funding public services in Europe.* London: Institute for Public Policy Research.

Royal Commission on Long-Term Care (1999) *With Respect to Old Age: Long term care – Rights and responsibilities.* London: The Stationary Office.

Saville-Smith, K, G Allan, G Newbold, B Calkin, N Parata, et al (1995) *In the Interests of Justice: An evaluation of criminal legal aid in New Zealand.* Wellington: Legal Services Board.

Schoen, C, and M Doty (2004) 'Inequities in access to medical care in five countries: findings from the 2001 Commonwealth Fund International Health Policy Survey.' *Health Policy* 67(3): 309–322.

Schoen, C, R Osborn, M Doty, M Bishop, J Peugh, et al (2007) 'Toward higher-performance health systems: Adults' health care experiences in seven countries, 2007.' *Health Affairs* 26(web exclusives): w717–w734, doi: 10.1377/hlthaff.26.6.w717.

Schoen, C, R Osborn, P Huynh, M Doty, K Davis, et al (2004) 'Primary care and health system performance: adults' experiences in five countries.' *Health Affairs* 23(web exclusives), w4–487–503.

'Scope of legislation of 1938' (no date) From *An Encyclopaedia of New Zealand,* edited by AH McLintock, originally published in 1966. *Te Ara: The Encyclopedia of New Zealand.* www.TeAra.govt.nz/en/1966/social-security/2 (updated 22 April 2009).

Secretary of State for Health (2008) *High Quality Care for All: NHS next stage review final report.* London: Department of Health.

Smith, J (2008) *Critical Analysis of the Implementation of the Primary Health Care Strategy and Framing of Issues for the Next Phase.* Wellington: Ministry of Health.

Smith, J (2009) 'Budget 09: Infants able to stay in early childhood centres for longer.' *New Zealand Herald* 29 May. www.nzherald.co.nz/jacqueline-smith/news/article.cfm?a_id=481&objectid=10575179 (accessed 15 March 2010).

'Social security: Health benefits' (no date) From *An Encyclopedia of New Zealand* edited by AH McLintock, originally published in 1966. *Te Ara: The Encyclopedia of New Zealand.* www.TeAra.govt.nz/en/1966/medical-services/20 (updated 22 April 2009, accessed 22 September 2008).

Statham, J (1997) 'Day care for children in need: Universal provision or a targeted service?' *Early Child Development and Care* 136(1): 1–15.

Tamblyn, R, R Laprise, JA Hanley, M Abrahamowicz, S Scott, et al (2008) 'Adverse events associated with prescription drug cost-sharing among poor and elderly persons.' *Journal of the American Medical Association* 285(4): 421–429.

UK Department of Health (2006) *Care Homes for Older People: National minimum standards and Care Homes Regulations 2001.* London: Stationary Office.

UK Department of Health (2009) *A Quick Guide to Help with Health Costs Including Charges and Optical Voucher Values. Effective from 1 April 2009.* London: Department of Health. www.dh.gov.uk/prod_consum_dh/groups/dh_digitalassets/documents/digit alasset/dh_099155.pdf (accessed 15 March 2010).

UK Department of Health (no date) *Charging for Social Care.* www.dh.gov.uk/en/SocialCare/Chargingandassessment/ChargingforSocial Care/index.htm (accessed 15 March 2010).

UK Parliament (2009) *Daily Hansard: Written ministerial statements – Family legal aid and legal aid reform.* www.publications.parliament.uk/pa/cm200809/cmhansrd/cm090720/wmst ext/90720m0004.htm (accessed 2 November 2009).

Victoria Legal Aid (2007) 'Country report: Australia.' Paper presented to the International Legal Aid Group Conference, Antwerp.

Wanless, D (2006) *Securing Good Care for Older People: Taking a long-term view.* Wanless Social Care Review. London: King's Fund.

Whitbread, N (1972) *The Evolution of the Nursery-Infant School.* London: Routledge and Kegan Paul.

Work and Income (2009) *Help with Childcare Costs: A guide for parents and caregivers.* Wellington: New Zealand Government. www.workandincome.govt.nz/documents/help-with-childcare-costs-alla0002.pdf (accessed 15 March 2010).

Work and Income (no date) *What Is a Residential Care Loan?* www.workandincome.govt.nz/manuals-and-procedures/income_support/extra_help/residential_care_loan/residential_ca re_loan-02.htm (accessed 15 March 2010).